Bellevue Timeline

The Story of Washington's Leading Edge City

From Homesteads to High Rises,

1863-2003

Bellevue Timeline

The Story of Washington's Leading Edge City
From Homesteads to High Rises, 1863-2003
by Alan J. Stein & the HistoryLink Staff

Designed by Marie McCaffrey, Crowley Associates, Inc.
Edited by Priscilla Long and Walt Crowley
Special Photography by Nick Gunderson
Principal Research by Alyssa Burrows
Supplemental Research by David Wilma

Special Thanks to Heather Trescases and Mary Ellen Piro, Eastside Heritage Center,
and Chris Smith Towne
Historical photographs courtesy of Eastside Heritage Center (EHC) or City of
Bellevue (COB) unless noted

Special funding provided by PACCAR Inc, the City of Bellevue, Paul & Henrietta
Vander Hoek, and the Bellevue 50Fest Sponsors

First Printing: March 2004
Produced by History Ink/HistoryLink
www.historylink.org
Distributed by the University of Washington Press
www.washington.edu/uwpress

To learn more about Bellevue, visit www.cityofbellevue.org and www.historylink.org

HistoryLink®

Bellevue
Timeline

The Story of Washington's Leading Edge City
From Homesteads to High Rises,
1863-2003

by Alan J. Stein & the HistoryLink Staff

Presented by

Special Photography by Nick Gunderson

In Memory of Lucile McDonald, Bellevue Historian

A HistoryLink Book

Produced for the City of Bellevue
Distributed by the University of Washington Press

Foreword

On a cold day early in the spring of 1953, civic leaders Phil Reilly and Eugene Boyd donned overcoats and fedoras to pose for a newspaper photographer next to a road marker reading "Bellevue Unincorporated." As Boyd steadied the signpost, Reilly reached up with a charred stick and crossed out the "Un" in Unincorporated. Bellevue had officially become a city on March 31, 1953.

Half a century later to the day, Gene Boyd's grandson and Phil Reilly's son recreated this marker of municipal birth in front of a cheering audience at Meydenbauer Center while leaders and citizens took turns imitating the late Phil Reilly's iconic vandalism. The event launched a yearlong "50Fest" celebration of Bellevue's evolution into a unique and important urban center of the Pacific Northwest.

These past 50 years have witnessed an astonishing transformation of what was a semi-rural community of fewer than 8,000 souls. As Bellevue began to grow through the 1950s and 1960s, former berry fields and clear cuts gave way to idyllic suburban subdivisions and one of the region's first shopping centers. Next came headquarters for major corporations such as PACCAR and Puget Sound Energy, auto dealerships, and regional distribution centers.

The city's low commercial costs helped to nurture fledgling start-ups such as a little software company called Microsoft (now based just northeast of town in Redmond), not to mention hundreds of other businesses large and small. Sound planning, superior schools, modern infrastructure, and a beautiful natural setting made Bellevue a magnet for families and residents of all ages and incomes.

The 1990s and first years of the new millennium brought both dramatic surges in employment and investment along with sudden downtowns and geopolitical shocks, but Bellevue weathered the turbulence better than most communities. The credit belongs to a tradition of public stewardship for both the environment

and society. Forward-looking planning has accommodated economic and population growth without jeopardizing neighborhood quality. A civic-minded and innovative business community has created tens of thousands of jobs and unlimited opportunity. Foremost, a dedicated, compassionate, and creative citizenry reflecting a wide diversity of cultures and backgrounds has taken pride in and responsibility for the community.

It is they who have made Bellevue the state's leading edge city and who continue to propel it forward as one of the region's most dynamic urban settings.

50Fest was just the latest manifestation of this community spirit and we salute the hundreds of citizen volunteers who brought life to an ambitious series of programs and events. We are grateful to the Eastside Heritage Center for planting the seed for this observance and to numerous local and regional businesses, institutions, and community organizations for providing financial and in-kind support.

This little book, which traces Bellevue's evolution from its first "Indian" residents to the latest immigrants from the real India, is offered as both a legacy of 50Fest and as an introduction and guide to our city. We hope it inspires you to learn more through Internet resources such as www.cityofbellevue.org and www.historylink.org online encyclopedia, and at the Eastside Heritage Center.

As proud as we are of our history, we believe that Bellevue's story has only just begun, and we welcome you to help write the chapters to come.

Connie Marshall, Mayor
Honorary 50Fest Co-Chair

Kemper Freeman Jr., Kemper Development Co.
Honorary 50Fest Co-Chair

Bellevue's Downtown Park provides an oasis of 20 landscaped acres linking the central business district with nearby Meydenbauer Bay (Gunderson)

The Present as Prologue

Before retracing Bellevue's past, it is helpful to consider the nature and character of the city today. If you ask people in Western Washington to describe Bellevue, most will conjure up an idealized vision of a 1950s suburban community with shopping centers, tidy ramblers, green lawns, and a white middle-class population that mostly works and plays somewhere else.

You can find such elements in Bellevue's past and in its present, but consider a few facts from the updated 2000 census:

- Fully one quarter of Bellevue's 117,000 residents are members of racial or ethnic minorities — about the same proportion of minorities as is found in Seattle.
- Bellevue businesses and institutions provide more than 130,000 jobs — more than twice as many as the number of employed city residents.

- Children in Bellevue Public Schools speak more than 50 native languages — and 25 percent of the city's population was not born in the United States.
- Nearly half of Bellevue residents occupy apartments, condominiums, or other multi-family housing — not suburban split-levels.
- Parks, trails, and protected open space cover 14 percent of Bellevue's land area, not counting more than 50 miles of, free-running streams that aid stormwater control and salmon migrations.

In short, Bellevue today is not what a lot of people imagine — or expect.

Bellevue at Home

Bellevue is a city of neighborhoods as diverse in form and style as might be found in any midsize urban community. Housing types range from high-rise apartments and condominiums in the city's bustling downtown to sylvan estates bordering on lakes and horse trails, with a diverse collection of housing choices in between.

The Cascades and I-90 floating bridges. Below: The growing community of Lakemont (Gunderson)

From the first day the Bellevue City Council met in April 1953, it has embraced a policy of active but intelligent growth. The City's first ordinance established a citizen planning commission, and Bellevue's comprehensive plans of the 1970s and 1980s provided models for Washington State's 1990 Growth Management Act.

Since 1953, the original city has multiplied in physical area to more than 31 square miles through a program of strategic annexations. At the same time, the city planned for higher densities which allowed the population to grow 16-fold over the past half-century without sacrificing the quality of life in Bellevue's numerous neighborhoods.

7

Bellevue Today

Bellevue City Limits   Major Parks   Other Parks

(Map labels: Lake Washington, Kirkland, Yarrow Point, Hunts Point, Clyde Hill, Medina, Bridle Trails, 148th NE, Redmond, Evergreen Highlands, North, Bel-Red/Northup, Red Rd, NE 24th St, NE 20th St, Northeast (Sammamish), Crossroads, NE 8th St, Downtown, Willburton, Main St, Southeast (Lake Hills), Lake Washington, Southwest, SE 8th St, Phantom Lake, Richards Valley, Beaux Arts, SE 24th St, Lake Sammamish, Eastgate, Mercer Island, Factoria, SE Newport Way, BELLEVUE, East Channel, Newcastle, Hilltop, Issaquah, Newport Hills, Coal Creek Way, Renton, Newcastle, Bellevue Way NE, Meydenbauer Bay)

BELLEVUE ANNEXATIONS

Since 1953, the original city has quintupled in physical area to more than 31 square miles through a program of strategic annexations.

Original Bellevue, 1953
1960 – 1979
1980 – 2004

(Map labels: Lake Washington, Original Bellevue, Lake Washington, 1960–1979, Lake Sammamish, 1980–2004, East Channel, 1980–2004)

The character of these varies dramatically. Within the original city limits, North Bellevue features larger homes and tree-lined streets dating from the 1950s and 1960s. This style is also found immediately south of downtown along Meydenbauer Bay and in neighborhoods such as Enatai amid some of the oldest surviving stands of timber in the city.

The original city limits also embrace the city's first planned residential development, Vuecrest, on Downey Hill. Downtown Bellevue's rising number of office and residential towers poses a dramatic urban counterpoint to these more traditional suburban communities, which are buffered from adverse development impacts through carefully graduated zoning. Bellevue's compact downtown neighborhood is slated to add some 11,000 housing units — three fourths of all projected new housing construction in the city limits — by 2020.

Right: Many Bellevue homes stand in mature forests. (Gunderson)

Heading East

As Bellevue expanded eastward toward the shores of Lake Sammamish in the 1960s, it embraced once remote communities south and east of Washington State's 431-acre Bridle Trails Park. This area is an equestrian Eden of large homes on spacious, wooded lots lining quiet streets and trails and includes the 160-acre Bellevue Golf Course.

Older neighborhoods on Wilburton Hill and in Richards Valley could trace their origins back to the first loggers, mill workers, and coal miners employed on the Eastside nearly a century and a half ago. At the same time, the city absorbed subdivisions built during the 1950s and 1960s in large part to help house Boeing's swelling workforce of engineers, managers, and skilled workers.

Lake Hills epitomizes the classic ramblers and tract planning of the 1950s. Smaller developments with such storybook monikers as Sherwood Forest, Chevy Chase, and Ardmore also lured young, middle-class homeowners by promising suburban serenity. The Highland community, which occupies a ridge around today's Crossroads shopping center, has offered smaller homes and apartments to growing numbers of middle and lower income families since the 1960s.

Growing South

Communities south of Interstate 90 began to join Bellevue in the 1980s. They reflect great contrasts in housing vintage and style. Older neighborhoods in the Newport Hills community such as Hazelwood once provided homes to the Northern European immigrants who worked Newcastle's coal mines. Plans for heavy industrial development gave Factoria its name, but only one stove and furnace maker ever

built there. Instead, homes sprang up on recently logged lands with romantic names such as Sunset Ravine, Woodridge Hill, Greenwich Crest, Mockingbird Hill, and Monthaven, while shopping centers and modern businesses took root where "hundreds of smokestacks" were supposed to rise.

Left: A young angler tries his luck in Phantom Lake. Above: Homes in south end neighborhoods enjoy easy access to downtown Bellevue, while the Bridle Trails area (below) offers sylvan seclusion (Gunderson)

To the east, the established Somerset neighborhood (annexed into Bellevue in the late 1960s at the same time as east Bellevue communities) shares ridgetop space with the growing Lakemont area community. This largely single family neighborhood is characterized by its denser "village" core, where shops, services and higher density housing absorb much of the growth that is attracted to Bellevue's south side. Both Somerset and Lakemont lie adjacent to the unincorporated areas of Hilltop and Eastgate. Hilltop developed first as a collaborative community, and Eastgate absorbed growth similar to

Tens of thousands of workers and shoppers fill downtown every day, while Meydenbauer Center (above) hosts concerts and conventions. Right: The King County Library's Bellevue Branch quenches Bellevueites' thirst for knowledge (Gunderson)

that found in east Bellevue and in Newport Hills. City planners expect both of these areas to join the city over the next few years.

Bellevue at Work

On a typical weekday, the population of Bellevue swells to more than 170,000 even as many depart for jobs elsewhere in the region. The city provides employment for more than 130,000 people, double the number of workers who call Bellevue home.

Bellevue's economic health is buttressed by a diversified economy, creative entrepreneurs, loyal businesses, savvy investors, and fiscally responsible and farsighted public policies. Its retail sales and property values exceed those of every other city in Washington except the far larger Seattle.

Bellevue is home to an extraordinary variety of businesses ranging from the international headquarters of PACCAR Inc — makers of world-renowned Kenworth, Peterbilt, DAF, and Foden trucks — and the region's largest private utility, Puget Sound Energy, to local craftspersons, art galleries, and backroom inventors. It boasts the most trend-setting shopping center in the Pacific Northwest, Bellevue Square, and some of Puget Sound's most prestigious auto dealers. It incubated many of the leading companies in the computer, Internet, and wireless telecom revolutions of the past decade, and more than 80 percent of Bellevue residents are "on line."

Not surprisingly, knowledge and education are premiums for the people of Bellevue, 54 percent of whom have earned at least a bachelor's degree (compared to 25 percent nationally and 40 percent in King County overall). Bellevue Public Schools and the Bellevue Community College are regarded as two of the finest such systems in the state, and residents are served by one of the

region's top private health care centers, Overlake Hospital. Thus, Bellevue offers employers a large and growing pool of highly educated and motivated employees, augmented in recent years by significant immigration from Asia and Latin America.

Despite a need for further state and federal transportation investments, Bellevue is well connected with other parts of the state and Pacific Northwest. Floating bridges across Lake Washington link Bellevue to Seattle, Puget Sound, and Interstate 5, while Interstate 90 is the state's main line across the Cascade Range. Interstate 405 serves north-south traffic between major Boeing facilities in greater Everett and Renton and the region's aviation gateway at Seattle-Tacoma International Airport. New hotels and convention facilities such as Meydenbauer Center have made Bellevue a regional conference hub. And, as the home of more than one out of ten King County jobs, Bellevue is no longer a "bedroom community."

Bellevue at Play

Bellevue's all-but-official motto is "a city in a park." Since 1953, the city has pursued an aggressive program of park acquisition and development combined with protection of wildlife habitats and open spaces. Major parks and greenbelts such as Mercer Slough, Kelsey Creek, Wilburton Hill and Bellevue Botanical Garden, and Weona Park are strung like pearls along

Fusao Kajima leads the Bellevue Philharmonic Orchestra.
A game of tag football in Robinswood Park (Gunderson)

an interlocking system of streams, trails, and pathways, and numerous neighborhood parks serve local needs.

The city's pioneering approach to storm drainage control has also preserved more than 50 miles of open streams, many of which are frequented by salmon on their way to and from Puget Sound and the Pacific beyond. For

terrestrial commuters, Downtown Park provides an oasis of 20 landscaped acres linking the central business district with nearby Meydenbauer Bay.

Those seeking more active recreation can find countless outlets at public parks and beaches and at private facilities such as the Bellevue Athletic Club. The award-winning Bellevue Branch of the King County Library System, the new Bellevue Art Museum and its annual arts fair, numerous performances at Meydenbauer Center, and concerts by the Bellevue Philharmonic Orchestra and the Bellevue Youth Symphony offer ample exercise for the mind and soul.

We hope this little introduction to modern Bellevue has piqued your curiosity about how the city came to be and to grow, because that begs a story — really many stories — that might also surprise you...

Bellevue Square is a mecca for holiday shoppers and families find winter fun at Downtown Park's seasonal skating rink (Gunderson)

The frame of a Coastal Salish longhouse, typical of those built by Bellevue's first residents, the Hah-tshu-ab'sh, or "lake people" (Edward S. Curtis, Library of Congress)

For centuries before 1850, Indians live in the vicinity of what is now Bellevue.

Isaac N. Ebey canoes into "Lake Washington" in 1850, in the first recorded visit by a white man.

Treaty of Point Elliott — the Duwamish and other tribes are forced to cede their land in 1855.

Following the "Battle of Seattle" in 1856, U.S. soldiers canoe to the site of Newport Shores and find abandoned Indian encampments.

Coal is discovered near Issaquah and Coal Creek in 1862.

Newcastle coal mines are operating in 1867.

10,000 BCE ~ 1882: First People

For thousands of years, the area we know today as Bellevue was inhabited by Salish Indians called the Hah-tshu-ab'sh, or "lake people" — so named for their proximity to the waters of Lake Washington and Lake Sammamish. The lake people spent their summers fishing, hunting, and harvesting berries and wapatos — a type of marsh tuber. In the wintertime, the people gathered in villages that dotted the lakeshores.

One of their larger settlements was a group of longhouses known as Sa'tsaka L, along Mercer Slough near present-day Factoria. A smaller longhouse stood near what is now Yarrow Bay, and it is believed that a cemetery was located along the northern tip of Meydenbauer Bay. Many of these sites were connected by trails that wended their way east to Snoqualmie Pass.

The first recorded visit to Lake Washington by a white man occurred in the summer of 1850, when Colonel Isaac Ebey made his way up the Duwamish River by canoe. Captivated by the beauty of the large body of water, he named it Lake Geneva. The name never took hold, and eventually it was named Lake Washington.

Culture Clash

In 1851, the first white settlers arrived in what was to become Seattle and were met by members of the Suquamish tribe who — mostly through the efforts of Chief Seattle — welcomed them with open arms. Indians living deeper in the foothills and east of the Cascade Mountains were more hesitant to embrace this change of worlds. When peace treaties were signed that ceded land from the Indians, some resorted to violence after whites encroached on treaty lands.

In January 1856, approximately 150 Indians attacked the village of Seattle. The settlers took cover, protected by the Navy sloop-of-war *Decatur* anchored in Elliott Bay. The attackers were repelled, and many of them traveled across Lake Washington to make camp at Sa'tsaka L, before returning to Eastern Washington.

That spring, Army troops and volunteers crossed Lake Washington and found the recently abandoned camp. Traveling eastward, many Seattleites got their first glimpse of the tree-lined hills and fertile wetlands between Lake Washington and Lake Sammamish. Some made a note of it, and told their friends when they returned home.

THE LAKE PEOPLE

For 12,000 years, the Hah-tshu-ab'sh lived on the shores of It-how-chug — today called Lake Washington. Their longhouses were built from large planks, and usually housed three to four families. These homes were built near the mouths of streams, where fish weirs were built.

Tribal members harvested wapatos along the shore, and berries along the hillsides. On a regular basis, the underbrush was burned to allow more sunlight into the forest, which facilitated berry growth. During waterfowl migration, hunters would go out on the lake at night in canoes. There were so many birds that they could easily be speared under the light of the moon.

The people believed in animal spirits, and knew that a lake monster lived close to Mercer Island, or Tlhah-chos. No one lived there, but deer were routinely driven off the mainland near Beaux Arts, and would be rounded up on the island. The Lake People knew best to leave by nightfall, lest they drown when the island was swallowed by the lake spirit after sundown.

Like many Puget Sound Indians, the Lake People suffered tragic losses during the smallpox epidemic in the 1770s. By the time the first white settlers arrived in Bellevue in the 1860s, most of the remaining Indians had been moved to reservations.

CLARK STURTEVANT

William Meydenbauer and Aaron Mercer were Bellevue's first pioneers, but stayed for only a short time. Clark Merrill Sturtevant followed after them and spent more than a quarter-century in the Bellevue vicinity.

Sturtevant was born in Vermont in 1840. After moving to Illinois with his family in 1848, he enlisted in the 112th infantry in 1862. When the Civil War ended, a law was passed granting veterans 160 acres of land for their service. Sturtevant moved west to stake his claim. He arrived in Washington in 1870 and moved to the Bellevue area in 1873.

Sturtevant chose property that is now bordered by NE 8th Street on the north, SE 8th Street on the south, 112th Avenue NE on the west, and 116th Avenue NE on the east. He trapped beaver, otter, and muskrat, and saved up enough money to buy more property, including a small body of water that became Lake Sturtevant. Today it is known as Lake Bellevue.

In 1890, Sturtevant married 17-year-old Florence Cleveland, whom some mistakenly believed was a niece of President Grover Cleveland. Ten years later they moved to Seattle, but at the time of his death in 1911, the Bellevue property was still in his name.

After the Indian attack, many settlers hesitated to stray far from Seattle. That changed in 1862, when Congress passed the Homestead Act, which allowed anyone who was head of a household and at least 21 years of age to claim a 160-acre parcel of land. Those who cleared 10 acres on their property, built a home, and lived in it could claim the land as their own after five years.

Soon people began moving east of Lake Washington. Farmland was good in the Squak Valley south of Lake Sammamish and coal had been discovered in the nearby mountains, so many homesteaders moved there first. Others explored the shores of Lake Washington, looking for a good place to build a cabin and work the land, initially choosing such spots as Juanita Bay and the mouth of the Sammamish River.

The future community of Bellevue got off to a slow start. It wasn't until 1869 that Seattle baker William Meydenbauer rowed across the lake and staked a claim in the cove that came to bear his name. He was only interested in building a summer home, and found that Indians often stole his windows while he was away.

The first "true" homesteaders were Aaron Mercer and his wife Ann, who settled along the western bank of a swampy waterway south of Meydenbauer's claim. Aaron was the younger brother of Seattle pioneers Thomas and Asa Mercer, and at the time he built his cabin, he and his wife had eight children. Within a few years, the family moved to a larger home south of Seattle, but the name Mercer Slough has remained ever since.

Seattle baker William Meydenbauer later had a bay named after him

Permanent Settlers

In 1873, Civil War veteran Clark Sturtevant built a cabin on what is now the corner of NE 8th Street and 116th Avenue. His property extended to Lake Sturtevant, now Lake Bellevue. In 1879, Seattle cabinetmaker John Zwiefelhofer acquired property north of Sturtevant. His commute involved hopping in a skiff and rowing it to Seattle and back, so he came home only on weekends, leaving his wife and children to clear the land.

Daniel Whitney's farm at Northup Way and 124th NE, 1887

The early 1880s saw the arrival of many new landowners, including Patrick Downey on the south slope of Clyde Hill, Albert Burrows in the Killarney area south of Meydenbauer Bay, and Matt and Lou Sharp, who claimed land in what is now downtown Bellevue alongside Isaac Bechtel Sr. and his family.

An informal post office was set up in Bechtel's cabin, and the mail was brought in by just about anyone making a trip to Seattle. Eventually, the government officially recognized the post office, which meant that a name was required. There are many tales as to how the name was chosen, but the most agreed-upon version tells that Matthew Sharp chose the name Bellevue, French for "beautiful view," because of the magnificent mountain vistas that lay to the east and west.

Aaron Mercer, the younger brother of Seattle pioneers Thomas and Asa Mercer

William Meydenbauer claims land on "Meydenbauer Bay" in spring 1869.

Aaron Mercer and Ann Stoven Mercer claim 80.5 acres along "Mercer Slough" in 1869.

The *James Mortie*, first power vessel on Lake Washington, arrives in 1870.

Clark Sturtevant claims land south of "Lake Bellevue" and traps mink and muskrat in 1873.

The Seattle & Walla Walla Railroad is completed from Renton to Newcastle in 1878.

W. H. Miller settles in the Beaux Arts area and Austrian cabinetmaker John Zwiefelhofer secures a 124-acre homestead near the present-day Safeway Distribution Center in 1879.

Benson Northup settles at the south end of Yarrow Bay in 1880.

Patrick Downey homesteads a 160-acre tract on Clyde Hill and builds a log cabin at 100th NE and NE 12th in 1882.

Matt and Lou Sharp homestead the site of the future downtown, and pioneers name the area Bellevue, French for "beautiful view," in 1882.

Isaac Bechtel Sr. buys land near the present downtown in 1882.

Oxen hauling logs over a skid road near Bellevue, 1880s. Inset: The Hans Miller cabin has remained in place for more than a century. Below: Otto Berndt farm at Phantom Lake

Albert Burrows settles in the Killarney area south of Meydenbauer Bay, and builds the first public school in 1883.

The Hans Miller Cabin, the oldest structure in Bellevue still located on its original site, is built in 1884 on the site of present-day Robinswood Park.

Edward F. Lee builds the *Squak* for Captain J. C. O'Conner, who begins ferry service in 1884.

Newcastle coal industry thrives from 1884-1898.

Isaac Bechtel's log cabin becomes the first post office and Bechtel is named postmaster on July 21, 1886.

Bellevue's population is 52 in 1886.

The original log-shack Highland School opens near NE 24th and 142nd NE in 1887.

The Seattle, Lakeshore, & Eastern Railroad arrives on the Eastside in 1888.

1883~1940:
The Changing Landscape

As more people moved to Bellevue, the landscape began to change. Trees were cut and stump farmers cleared the land. Skid roads lined the hillsides and ox teams hauled logs to the water. Meydenbauer Bay was often so full of timber that it was almost possible to walk across it.

Cabins dotted the hills as far east as Phantom Lake – so named for its wisps of fog that sometimes took on human shapes. One of the first pioneers at Phantom Lake was Henry Thode, who moved there in 1883. For years, his closest neighbor was five miles away. Besides operating a small farm with his family, Thode hunted nearby for grouse and bear. He also dug a new outlet for the lake

so that it drained toward Lake Sammamish instead of into Kelsey Creek.

In 1884, Hans Miller built a cabin on the site of present-day Robinswood Park. This is the oldest structure in Bellevue still standing in its original location. The Daniel Fraser cabin built in 1888 in the Northup area is also extant, but has been moved to Kelsey Creek Park.

More families on the Eastside meant more children, and a need for schools. In 1883, Albert Burrows built Bellevue's first school in Killarney near what is now Chesterfield Park. His daughter Calanthia was the town's first teacher. In 1887, the Highland School was built, followed by a school at Northup.

Three years after Washington became a state in 1889, Bellevue held its first bond issue to construct a two-room schoolhouse with a bell tower at the corner of 100th NE and Main Street. Until 1909, high school students attended classes in Seattle.

Getting Around

Settlers sometimes traveled across the lake aboard the *Squak*, a 42-foot flat-bottomed boat captained by J. C. O'Connor. After 1890, getting to and from Bellevue became easier when the steamboat *C. C. Calkins* began making regular trips across Lake Washington from Leschi to Mercer Island to Meydenbauer Bay. Two years later, John Anderson, a deckhand aboard the boat, began his own passenger ferry service.

Main Street School, 1890s. Inset: Albert Burrows and Calanthia Burrows. Below: Settlers traveled across the lake aboard vessels like the Squak *and the steamer* C. C. Calkins

21

Daniel Fraser builds a log cabin in the Northup area in 1888 (moved to Kelsey Creek Park in 1974).

Charles Calkins launches the *C.C. Calkins*, a 74-foot passenger boat, on March 21, 1890.

Ove and Mary Larsen homestead the area east of 148th NE and north of SE 8th in 1890.

Isabel Bechtel takes over as postmistress on November 15, 1890, after her husband's death.

Washington Territory becomes a state on November 11, 1889.

D. M. Shanks plats the Cheriton Fruit Gardens tract on the site of present-day Bellevue Square in 1891.

Captain John Anderson begins the first scheduled ferry service between Bellevue and Seattle's Leschi Park in 1892.

Bellevue's first bond issue after statehood funds the two-room Bellevue Main Street School on 100th NE and Main in 1892.

22

May Johnson delivered the mail to Bellevue pioneers

Bellevue's first doctor, Charles M. Martin, begins practicing in 1892.

Mrs. Sam Belote names Medina after the holy city of Arabia in 1892.

Bellevue's first religious organization, the Union Sunday School, forms and meets in the Bellevue Schoolhouse in 1892.

A nationwide financial Depression occurs – the Panic of 1893.

W. W. Powell dams "Duey Creek," flowing into the slough at Wilburton, to form a log storage pond in 1894.

William Ivey becomes postmaster in 1894.

In 1895, mail arrives at Houghton by boat twice a week and May Johnson carries it by horse to Bellevue.

The First Community Church (renamed Bellevue Congregational Church) incorporates on May 4, 1896.

The first Japanese pioneers, Jusaburo Fuji and Mr. Setsuda, arrive in 1898.

Bellevue residents traveled around the community primarily on foot. May Johnson, a Prussian immigrant, carried mail from Houghton to Bellevue on horseback twice a week. She was paid $50 a year for this duty, and carried a can of pepper to ward off animal attackers.

The Seattle, Lake Shore & Eastern Railroad served other, faster-growing, eastside communities. Originally, the city of Kirkland was poised to become the hub of the Eastside with the planned construction of Peter Kirk's steel mill, but the Panic of 1893 brought an end to that venture. Nevertheless, Kirkland established an infrastructure early on, and initially grew at a faster rate than Bellevue. To the southeast, the communities of Newcastle and Issaquah were bustling due to rich seams of coal discovered years before.

Around 1903, the Hewitt-Lea Mill was built at the northern end of Mercer Slough, and part of the slough was converted into a log storage pond. The Northern Pacific Railroad – which had bought out the SLS&E line in 1898 – built a line through Midlakes, providing easier shipment of supplies from Seattle. The beltline connected Renton, Bellevue, Kirkland, and Woodinville, and one of its most striking features was the Wilburton trestle completed near the mill in 1904.

King County launched regular ferry service on Lake Washington in 1900, but for years John Anderson's private vessels thwarted this effort by scooping up passengers minutes before the county ferry arrived at the dock. The County sued Anderson for this practice, but later hired him as superintendent during a period of financial straits. No one knew how to operate a ferry system better than he.

Seattle, Lake Shore & Eastern locomotive, D. H. Gilman, ca. 1888

THE MILL BY THE SLOUGH

The Hewitt-Lea lumber mill was located near where Interstate 405 crosses SE 8th Street. When the mill was built in 1903, the waters of Mercer Slough were high enough for milled logs to be floated out on scows into Lake Washington, but only during winter months. In 1904, the Wilburton trestle was built overhead, and two years later a spur line was built up the Kelsey Creek Valley to various logging camps deep in the woods.

Many mill workers lived on the nearby hillside in the community of Wilburton, which by 1910 boasted a population of more than 350, as well as a grocery store, a pool hall, and a few saloons. Single men lived in bunkhouses, and families lived in cottages. Their children attended Wilburton school.

During its years of operation, Hewitt-Lea shipped more than a hundred million board feet of milled lumber through the slough. By 1916, most nearby trees had been cut down, but the mill's demise is linked to the opening of the Lake Washington Ship Canal and the Montlake Cut, which lowered the lake by nine feet, effectively turning Mercer Slough into a boggy swamp.

The Hewitt-Lea Lumber Company sued King County for this, and after much legal wrangling, received $125,000 in damages. In 1919, the school closed, and in 1923 the grocery store burned down. When highway 2-A (later I-405) was built beginning in the 1940s, it eliminated practically any remaining trace of the once-thriving logging community.

The census counts about 400 people in the vicinity of Bellevue in 1900.

Roads are constructed from Bellevue to Wilburton to Newport and from Bellevue to Medina in 1900.

Japanese begin clearing land for farming in 1900.

The First Community Church dedicates Bellevue's first church building in 1901.

Wilbur and England locate their logging operation at the upper end of Mercer Slough in 1901.

A road from Bellevue to Enatai opens in 1902.

Bellevue Lumber Co. takes over the Wilbur and England logging camp in 1903, with Wilbur as a business partner.

Wilburton timber railroad trestle opens in 1904.

Oliver Franz and William Raine plat Bellevue in 1904.

Sakutaro Takami plants Bellevue's first strawberry fields in 1904 at 102nd NE and NE 15th.

Timeline

A Thriving, Prosperous Suburb

First Baptist Church

By 1900, more than 400 people lived in the greater Bellevue community, with 100 people living near Meydenbauer Bay, 100 more living in Killarney, and 200 living near Medina, The Points, and Clyde Hill. Some of these residents were Japanese immigrants farming land that had been cleared of timber. In 1898, Jusaburo Fuji and Mr. Setsuda were the first Japanese to arrive, and in 1904 Sakutaro Takami planted the town's first strawberry fields at 102nd Avenue NE and NE 15th Street.

For years, local religious organizations had been meeting in places like the schoolhouse or in private homes, and in 1901 the town welcomed its first house of worship when the First Community Church was built at the corner of NE 8th and 108th NE. The First Baptist Church building, constructed in 1905 near NE 8th and 100th NE and later moved to 315 100th NE, is still standing.

In 1908, the Village of Beaux Arts was established as an artists' colony, making it the area's first planned residential community. Two general stores served the entire Bellevue community – McGauvran's General Merchandise Store on Main Street, and Godsey's at Midlakes. By 1910, 1,500 people lived in the greater Bellevue area.

Northern Pacific Railroad completes the Lake Washington Beltline in 1904 to connect Renton, Bellevue, Kirkland, and Woodinville.

The First Baptist Church organizes and constructs a bulding in 1905. The church is later moved to 315 100th NE.

Kinpachiro Furukawa organizes the first Japanese community cooperative in 1905.

After a violent disagreement, Wilbur dissolves his partnership with Henry Hewitt, and the Hewitt-Lea Lumber Co. acquires his interest in 1905.

Mary M. Gruber sells the Wilburton School property to School District No. 49 for $250 in 1906.

"Whoopie Road" (so nicknamed for its steep short hills) is constructed at 100th NE from Lake Washington north to NE 24th in 1906.

Fred J. Eitel plats Lochlaven in 1906.

The Wildwood Park Dance Hall, now Meydenbauer Bay Yacht Club, is built in 1906.

The Japanese food co-op expands to include farm supplies in 1907.

A road opens in 1907 at 108th NE from NE 24th south to SE 34th.

A lone telephone line reaches Medina in 1907.

Bellevue's first grocery and hardware store, corner of Main and 100th NE, 1917

Electricity and telephone service arrived. Improvement clubs, social organizations, and fraternal societies filled the needs of forward-thinking Bellevueites. Promotional brochures urged people to move to this "thriving, prosperous suburb of Seattle," and partake of "plenty of pure air and an abundance of the purest water (but no saloons)."

The ferry Leschi *in Meydenbauer Bay, as seen from Wildwood Park, 1910s. Below: Main Street School classroom, 1910 (UW Libraries)*

Cars and Boats

By the 1910s, automobiles had become the preferred mode of transportation, and dirt roads replaced footpaths and trails. In 1913, the auto ferry *Leschi* began service between Bellevue and Leschi Park in Seattle. The next year, the Bellevue Improvement Club formed to foster good roads and other community improvements, and in 1919, George Hanson opened a garage on Main Street.

The Village of Beaux Arts is established as an artists' colony in 1908.

Roads open at 104th NE from Main Street to Kirkland, and from Midlakes (116th NE) south to Newport in 1908.

Patrick McGauvran's Bellevue Mercantile Co. opens on the north side of Main Street, west of 102nd, in 1908.

Main Street School adds high school classes in 1909.

A road opens from 76th NE, Medina, north to Evergreen Point in 1909.

Greater Bellevue's population is 1,500 in 1910.

The Medina Grocery store opens in 1910.

George Hanson's Auto Garage, 1920s

In 1915, Bellevue got its first high-tech industry when Eugene Sherman started the Dirigo Compass Factory and began shipping compasses and binnacles all over the world. The business community was changing, as the days of large-scale logging were coming to an end. In 1916, the Hewitt-Lea Mill, which had once cut 20,000 board feet of lumber per day, found itself high and dry when the construction of the Lake Washington Ship Canal and the subsequent opening of the Montlake Cut lowered Lake Washington by about nine feet and turned Mercer Slough into a bog.

The ship canal provided direct access from Lake Washington to Puget Sound, charting a new future for Bellevue and the Eastside. The first benefit of the ship canal was a new business in Bellevue, seemingly incongruous for the rural community — a whaling fleet. Local resident William Schupp, head of the American Pacific Whaling Fleet, was looking for a place to moor his boats during the winter months. He chose Meydenbauer Bay because Lake Washington's fresh water helped kill off barnacles and worms that damaged salt-water vessels.

Dirigo Compasses and Binnacles
"Detroit" on her remarkable voyage to St. Petersburg used the identical Dirigo compass which so successfully guided the "Sea Bird" across the Atlantic. Can you ask for a stronger indorsement? Write today for catalog. If your dealer cannot supply you I will send one on approval, express paid.
Manufactured by
EUGENE M. SHERMAN, Box 6 Bellevue, P. O. Seattle, Washington
Eastern Distributors—Canadian-Fairbanks Co., Montreal, St. John, Ottawa, Toronto. Wm. H. Whiting & Co., Baltimore, Md.

Checking the harpoon cannon aboard a whaling vessel in Meydenbauer Bay, ca. 1925

The Terumatsu Yabuki family at Yarrow Point, ca. 1935. Below: Mutsuo Hashiguchi holds his son Lester in the strawberry fields.

Down on the Farms

By the 1920s, the stumps had been removed near downtown Bellevue, exposing fertile land throughout the area. More people took to cultivating crops, but the economic competition with Japanese immigrants who had been farming much of the land since 1900 caused friction within the community. In 1921, the Washington Alien Land Law Act was passed, which prevented Issei (first generation Japanese Americans) from owning land.

That same year, a Japanese Language School was closed for four years due to racial unrest, when some felt that the schools were being used to indoctrinate Nisei (second gen-eration Japanese Americans) into forced loyalty towards Japan and its emperor. These rumors were unfounded, but coincided with a growing wave of anti-Japanese sentiment that was building all along the West Coast.

Largely due to E. E. Webster's efforts, Bellevue's first telephone service begins in 1914.

The Nihonjinkai (Japanese Community Association) is organized in 1914.

The Bellevue Improvement Club is formed in 1914.

The town of Medina is platted and recorded in 1914.

A road opens on 120th NE from Bellevue to Redmond in 1914.

A timber bridge is built over Meydenbauer ravine on what is now NE 1st in 1915.

Eugene Sherman starts the Dirigo Compass Factory on NE 1st just west of 100th NE in 1915.

Between July and October 1916, digging the Montlake Cut for the Lake Washington Ship Canal lowers Lake Washington 8.8 feet and drains much of Mercer Slough. The Hewitt-Lea Lumber Co. later sues King County for $125,000 in damages, and wins on appeal to the Washington State Supreme Court.

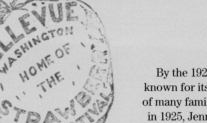

IT'S THE BERRIES!

By the 1920s, Bellevue had become well known for its tasty strawberries, a chief crop of many families, mostly Japanese. One night in 1925, Jenny Bovee had a dream about a celebration featuring the strawberry harvest. She told her husband Charles, a local realtor and later Bellevue's first mayor, who thought it was a great idea. A committee was formed, and $40 was raised to pay for the first festival, which attracted 3,000 visitors.

Word spread, and over the years more and more people came to nosh on yummy shortcakes drenched in strawberries and cream, while watching skits and acts performed on stage. Car caravans would travel from nearby cities as a show of neighborly support.

In 1935, more than 15,000 people attended the festival — nearly five times the number of people living in the small town. The three-day event continued to be held annually until 1942, the year 55 local Japanese families were forced to go to internment camps. Most of Bellevue's strawberries at that time were grown by Japanese farmers, who cultivated 472 acres in and around Bellevue.

In 1987, the Bellevue Historical Society revived the Strawberry Festival to honor the city's past. Since then, it has once again become an annual tradition, enjoyed by many from all walks of life.

You Are Invited To Atte

LAKE WASHINGTO

STRAWBERRY FES

AT BELLEVUE

3 Days-Friday, Saturday

JUNE 19, 2

Fill Up on Hot Strawberry

Philip Hennig sneaking some grapes from the family business, 1925. Below: The Lake Washington Reflector *provided hometown news.*

Nevertheless, many Bellevue residents considered their Japanese neighbors as friends, and employed them on their farms because of their agricultural expertise. There were many farms throughout the community, including ones that produced lettuce, apples, poultry, milk, grapes, rabbits, and even mink fur. But most of all, Bellevue became known far and wide as a center for tasty strawberries.

In 1925, Bellevue held its first Strawberry Festival on Main Street, and attracted nearly 3,000 visitors – more visitors than residents of the town. Many who came to the annual festivals liked what they saw, and some ended up moving to the Eastside.

Signs of Growth

Bellevue was acquiring all the accoutrements of small town living. Dozens of businesses dotted Main Street. Beginning in 1918, W. Eugene LeHuquet published a weekly news-

To honor three local men killed in World War I, the Bellevue Minute Women plant three elm trees in front of the Bellevue Grade School in January 1920.

The Bellevue District Development Club incorporates in April 1920.

Washington Alien Land Law Act, forbidding Japanese from purchasing land, is enacted on March 2, 1921.

The Japanese Language School temporarily closes in 1921 due to acts of prejudice and discrimination.

The Bellevue Women's Club is organized in 1922.

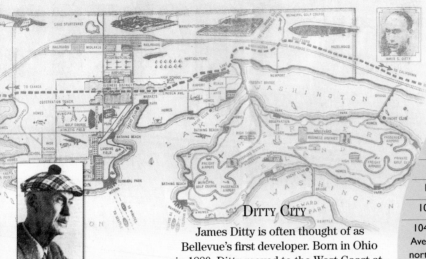

Memory Lanes

Before Bellevue adopted a numerical street grid in the 1930s, downtown streets bore names chosen by early landowners as they platted their holdings, including:

100th ➤ Wildwood Avenue

102nd ➤ Linden Avenue

103rd ➤ Connor Avenue

104th (now Bellevue Way) ➤ Lincoln Avenue south of Main, Peach Avenue north of Main

105th ➤ Lucerne Avenue

106th ➤ Lomond Avenue

107th ➤ Rainier Avenue

SE 8th ➤ Cleveland Street

SE 6th ➤ Alder Street (Mountain View Road between 106th and 107th)

SE 3rd ➤ Cedar Street

Main St ➤ St. James Road west of 104th, Otto Rhetteplace Road east of 104th

NE 2nd ➤ Charles Street

NE 3rd ➤ Stetson Street

NE 4th ➤ Cherry Avenue (NE 6th was created later)

NE 8th ➤ Redmond-Bellevue Road

Before rezoning, several roads cut diagonally through the future downtown, including Kilmarnock Road, Cliff Place, and Afton Place. The original Bellevue Way was a shortcut between 100th SE and Main Street. (Source: 1943 Kroll Atlas of Seattle)

DITTY CITY

James Ditty is often thought of as Bellevue's first developer. Born in Ohio in 1880, Ditty moved to the West Coast at the age of 24, where he found work as a press photographer. In 1910 he bought a home in the fledgling arts community of Beaux Arts, south of Meydenbauer Bay.

At the time, Bellevue was essentially a crossroads with a store or two, but Ditty predicted that one day more than 200,000 people would call the Eastside their home. In 1928, he began buying up land north of Main Street — a venture his friends thought was foolish, the more so after the Great Depression hit hard the following year.

As Ditty stated years later, "I sat on the fence waiting for Bellevue to grow up. Everybody gave me the horse laugh." Friends chuckled louder when he drew up a plan for Bellevue that included skyscrapers, hotels, and a series of bridges across the lake — a plan which *Seattle Times* illustrator Sam Groff made fun of in cartoons by naming the town of tomorrow "Ditty City."

Ditty was upset at the name, because he was serious about his vision. In the late 1940s he began selling parcels of his land, including 10 acres to Kemper Freeman for the construction of Bellevue Square. Throughout the 1950s, Ditty sold more downtown property, but only for commercial use. Ditty died in 1962 at the age of 81, just as Bellevue was becoming the city of which he'd always dreamed.

Evening English and homemaking classes for the Japanese begin at Hunts Point in 1922.

The wooden East Channel Bridge connecting Mercer Island and the east shore of Lake Washington at Enatai opens in 1923.

The Japanese Consulate formally dedicates the Bellevue Japanese Community Association in 1923.

The first annual Strawberry Festival is held behind the Main Street School in mid-June 1925.

Charles Bovee founds Bellevue Realty in 1925.

The Japanese Language School re-opens at Downey Hill (98th NE and NE 9th) in 1925.

Bellevue Women's Club members start first public library in the "lunch room building" — also known as McGauvran's building — on Main and 100th NE on November 12, 1925.

Construction of the Sacred Heart Church begins at 108th NE and Main on March 3, 1926.

After four fires in one month, *Reflector* editor W. E. LeHuquet publishes first appeal for a fire department in 1926.

Looking south on what would become the corner of Bellevue Way and NE 8th, ca. 1925. Below: Commander Miller Freeman, 1918

paper, *The Lake Washington Reflector,* out of his home. *The East Side Journal*, a Kirkland weekly, also carried Bellevue news. In 1925, the Bellevue Women's Club opened the town's first library, composed of 300 discards from the Seattle library, a box of books from the Washington State Library, and a few volumes donated by residents.

In 1928, Lincoln Avenue (later named Bellevue Way) was paved from Main Street to NE 8th Street, and opened as a county arterial. Until this time, the commercial district lay primarily on Main Street, but that soon changed. James Ditty bought up land along Lincoln Avenue hoping to set up a town center north of Main. It was also during this time that Miller Freeman and his family moved to Groat Point, beginning a legacy of downtown development that would last to this day.

A stone World War I monument is dedicated on November 11, 1926, near the memorial elms planted in 1920.

The first Japanese Nisei marriage is held — Takeo Matsuoka and Kazue Hirotaka — in 1926.

The Sacred Heart Church building is completed in 1926.

John Larson donates a small building for the Bellevue Library at Main and 103rd in 1927.

Bellevue's first golf course, the 18-hole Overlake Golf Club in the Medina area, opens on May 7, 1927, with membership limited to 300, including many Seattleites.

The Japanese Youth Club — Seinenkai — is organized with about 25 members in 1927.

Lincoln Avenue (now Bellevue Way) is paved from Main to NE 8th in 1928.

Miller Freeman and family move from Seattle to a 14-room mansion on Groat Point on June 24, 1928.

Meta's Drug Store was a favorite gathering place for more than half a century. Below: Highland Dairy truck

James S. Ditty acquires some 40 acres along Lincoln in 1928.

The Frederick Winters House is built in 1929.

The Japanese Language School at 88th NE and NE 18th (Eastland) opens, and Mr. Asaichi Tsushima becomes the first teacher in 1929.

Union S High School, Bellevue's first high school, opens on 102nd NE between NE 1st and NE 4th in 1930.

Wright's Barber Shop opens at 10251 Main in 1930.

Jane McDowell's Candies opens in 1930.

The *Bellevue American* newspaper debuts on July 10, 1930.

The "Kokaido," the Japanese Community Association Clubhouse, opens at 102nd NE and NE 10th and holds Buddhist and Christian services in 1930.

When the Great Depression hit in 1929, Bellevue weathered it better than most communities. There were no big industries to lay off workers, and farm produce such as berries, eggs, and milk remained valuable commodities. Nearby Medina, where many Seattle business moguls had summer homes, suffered worse. The Overlake Golf Club, a private club that opened in 1927, was foreclosed and shut down in 1935.

Even though times were tough for Bellevue residents during the Depression, the little town continued to grow, albeit slowly. The Union S High School was built in 1930, and that same year the *Bellevue American* newspaper started publication. Small businesses started up, including Meta's

Drug Store, run by Meta Burrows. She also housed the liquor store, now that Prohibition had ended. And in 1939, Bellevue got its first supermarket, the Lakeside Supermarket at 104th NE and NE 8th.

Bridge to the Future

Transportation remained an issue for the tiny community. The Lake Washington Ferry system was the predominant form of travel to and from Seattle, although crude roads circled the lake. The East Channel Bridge was built between Enatai and Mercer Island in 1923, but that still left lots of lake on the other side of the island.

In town, few roads were paved. Bridges were built over ravines, and dirt streets laced through downtown in a grid system. During the Depression, the federal Works Progress Administration helped build more roads, trails, and beach access throughout the Eastside.

But the most expensive, innovative, and dramatic change to Eastside transportation was the construction of the Lake Washington Floating Bridge, which opened in 1940. Now, for the price of a small toll, people could live in Bellevue and commute by car to Seattle. The bridge would have killed the ferry system outright, if not for the start of World War II.

Phyllis Hill and Ted McCreary enjoying a swim in Meydenbauer Bay. Left: Lake Washington Floating Bridge brochure, 1940

The Bellevue Growers Association is organized in 1930.

The Pacific Telephone and Telegraph Company lays 75 tons of lead-sheathed submarine cable across Lake Washington in 1931.

The Furuya Bank goes bankrupt and many Issei lose their life savings in 1932.

Lake Washington Boulevard is paved from Kirkland to Renton in 1932.

The Japanese Packing Plant, a cooperative storage shed for Japanese American farmers, is built at 11660 NE 8th in 1933.

W. B. Sydnor plants about five acres of blueberries on 106th NE in 1933.

Pharmacist Meta Jacobson Burrows opens Meta's Drug Store on Main and Linden (now 102nd NE) in the old bank building in 1934.

The *Reflector's* last issue appears in December 1934.

Fire destroys Schupp's whaling dock on March 1, 1935.

The Works Progress Administration (WPA) builds trails, a road, log shelters, and a park for public access to Meydenbauer Bay in 1935.

After rejecting proposed public use to pay its bills, Overlake Golf Club closes on April 30, 1935.

The Bellevue Library moves into the Bellevue Clubhouse, a block north of Main on 100th in 1935.

The Department of Highways advertises for bids for a bridge to cross Lake Washington, and engineer Homer Hadley proposes a floating concrete-pontoon bridge at a cost of $4.18 million in 1937.

Construction begins on the first floating bridge across Lake Washington on December 29, 1938.

Expanded to three days, the annual Strawberry Festival draws 10,000-15,000 visitors in 1939.

The Lakeside Supermarket opens at the southeast corner of 104th NE, (now Bellevue Way) and NE 8th in 1939.

The Lacey V. Murrow Floating Bridge opens and Governor Clarence Martin pays the first toll on July 2, 1940.

The Lake Washington Floating Bridge was hailed as a modern marvel

1941~1953: War and Peace

World War II led to a temporary but large increase in Eastside population. War workers were needed at the Lake Washington Shipyards in Houghton, as well as at Boeing in Seattle. The new floating bridge and the aging Lake Washington ferries were filled both ways each day with workers on their way to build ships and planes.

Thousands on the Eastside worked feverishly to support the troops and to guard the home front. A watchtower was built on Downey Hill so that plane spotters could keep an eye out for enemy aircraft. Victory gardens were planted, scrap metal was gathered, bond rallies were held.

Meanwhile, up and down the West Coast, tens of thousands of Japanese Americans were ordered out of their homes and sent to internment camps. Before the war, 55

Arthur A. Nordhoff founds Bellevue Airfield east of 156th SE and north of Sunset Highway (now Interstate 90) in 1941.

Overlake Elementary School building on 102nd NE opens in 1942.

Bellevue undergoes a test air-raid drill on January 4, 1942.

Lookouts begin from an airplane watchtower built on Clyde Hill in 1942.

Federal Executive Order 9066 sends some 300 local Japanese Americans to internment camps on May 20, 1942.

15 MINUTES
EXPRESS
to your HOME in the country

Japanese families farmed a total of 472 acres in Bellevue. After 1942, they were all gone. When the war ended in 1945, only a few returned.

Overall, the Bellevue community felt remorse for the loss of their Japanese neighbors and friends. But there were some who signed a petition protesting those Japanese who wished to come home. When war hero Kiyo Tabuki — who had enlisted in the U.S. Army and was wounded in both legs — brought his uniform to a Bellevue cleaner, he was turned away. The Japanese persisted against these occasional outbreaks of intolerance.

Square Dealers

Following the war, Bellevue began its transformation from a small town into a bustling suburban city. In 1946, Kemper Freeman Sr. opened Bellevue Square, with financial assistance from his father, Miller Freeman. Miller also owned a controlling interest in the *Bellevue American* newspaper, and he and his son along with eight other investors founded Bellevue's First National Bank.

Below: Bellevue civil defense volunteer first aid unit, 1942. Right: Winifred Evans Schafer and Violet Cort Schafer cover their ears during an air-raid drill, 1942

Bellevue cancels the strawberry festival in June 1942.

The Overlake School District consolidates local school districts in 1942.

The King County Library System, with head librarian Marguerite Groves, begins running the library in February 1944.

Water District No. 68 absorbs Bellevue Water Co. in 1946.

Bel-Vue Theatre opens with *Doll Face* on March 10, 1946.

Timeline

Freeman Sr. was instrumental in the creation of the Overlake School District, which consolidated Bellevue, Medina, Hunts Point, Highland, Factoria, Phantom Lake, and Union S districts.

The Freemans were by no means alone in the business community. James Ditty, John L. Scott, and others were developing and selling acres of downtown property to business owners, many of whom were members of the Bellevue Chamber of Commerce. The Chamber formed in 1947 out of the Bellevue District Development Club and the Bellevue Business Men's Association. Its first president was Harry Grant.

In this flurry of activity, Bellevue Square was the centerpiece of downtown commerce. The first business to open there was the 560-seat Bel-Vue Theatre, constructed with government-approved lumber as a morale booster at the end of the war. Frederick & Nelson was the first

36

Anti-Japanese flier, 1946

CASUALTIES OF WAR

Japan's bombing of Pearl Harbor in December 1941 set in motion a series of events and decisions that led to what has been called the worst violation of constitutional rights in American history: the expulsion and imprisonment of 110,000 persons of Japanese ancestry from the U.S. West Coast. More than 300 were from Bellevue, made up of 55 families of men, women, and children.

On May 20, 1942, these 55 families boarded trains in Kirkland, not knowing where they were heading. First they were taken to a temporary assembly center in Pinedale, California, and later they were moved to a permanent camp at Minidoka, Idaho, where they remained until the war's end in 1945.

The families at Minidoka suffered through below-zero winters and 115-degree summers, living in crude barracks averaging 16 x 20 feet in size. Some Nisei men volunteered for military service, and served with distinction in the Army's segregated 442nd Regimental Combat Team. These men hoped that it would improve their families' status after the war, but in many cases it did not.

Only 11 families returned to Bellevue after the war. Many citizens welcomed them back, but a more vocal minority of Bellvueites heaped them with scorn. The wounds of World War II took years to heal.

Kemper Freeman Sr. opens Bellevue Square on August 20, 1946.

The Food Center opens on August 23, 1946.

The Meydenbauer Bay Yacht Club opens in late summer 1946.

Miller and Kemper Freeman and others start the First National Bank in 1946.

Miller Freeman buys a 75% interest in the *Bellevue American* newspaper, and hires former owner A. J. Whitney to run it in 1946.

Bellevue Chamber of Commerce forms on January 21, 1947.

Carl Pefley organizes the first Arts & Crafts Fair in front of his Crabapple restaurant in July 1947.

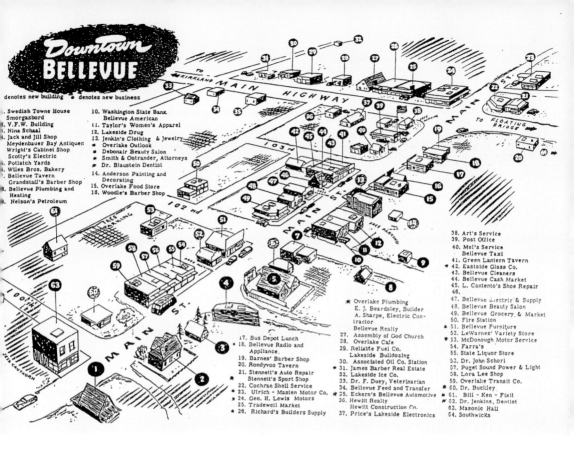

Downtown BELLEVUE

denotes new building • denotes new business

1. Swedish Towne House
   Smorgasbord
2. V.F.W. Building
3. Nina Schaal
4. Jack and Jill Shop
   Meydenbauer Bay Antiques
   Wright's Cabinet Shop
   Scotty's Electric
5. Potlatch Yards
6. Wiles Bros. Bakery
7. Bellevue Tavern
   Grandstaff's Barber Shop
8. Bellevue Plumbing and
   Heating
9. Nelson's Petroleum

10. Washington State Bank
    Bellevue American
11. Taylor's Women's Apparel
12. Lakeside Drug
13. Jenkin's Clothing & Jewelry
  • Overlake Outlook
  • Debonair Beauty Salon
  • Smith & Ostrander, Attorneys
  ✱ Dr. Blaustein Dentist
14. Anderson Painting and
    Decorating
15. Overlake Food Center
16. Woodle's Barber Shop

17. Bus Depot Lunch
• 18. Bellevue Radio and
    Appliance
19. Barnes' Barber Shop
20. Rondyvoo Tavern
21. Stennett's Auto Repair
    Stennett's Sport Shop
22. Cochran Shell Service
• 23. Ulrich - Masten Motor Co.
✱ 24. Geo. H. Lewis Motors
25. Tradewell Market
• 26. Richard's Builders Supply

✱ Overlake Plumbing
   E. J. Beardsley, Builder
   A. Sharpe, Electric Con-
   tractor
   Bellevue Realty
27. Assembly of God Church
28. Overlake Cafe
29. Reliable Fuel Co.
    Lakeside Bulldozing
30. Associated Oil Co. Station
• 31. James Barber Real Estate
32. Lakeside Ice Co.
33. Dr. F. Duey, Veterinarian
34. Bellevue Feed and Transfer
✱ 35. Eckern's Bellevue Automotive
36. Hewitt Realty
    Hewitt Construction Co.
37. Price's Lakeside Electronics

38. Art's Service
39. Post Office
40. Mel's Service
    Bellevue Taxi
41. Green Lantern Tavern
◀ 42. Eastside Glass Co.
43. Bellevue Cleaners
44. Bellevue Cash Market
45. L. Contento's Shoe Repair
46.
47. Bellevue Electric & Supply
48. Bellevue Beauty Salon
49. Bellevue Grocery & Market
50. Fire Station
• 51. Bellevue Furniture
52. LeWarnes' Variety Store
✱ 53. McDonough Motor Service
54. Farra's
55. State Liquor Store
56. Dr. John Schori
57. Puget Sound Power & Light
58. Lora Lee Shop
59. Overlake Transit Co.
• 60. Dr. Buckley
• 61. Bill - Ken - Fixit
✱ 62. Dr. Jenkins, Dentist
63. Masonic Hall
64. Southwicks

anchor store at the mall, and the Kandy Kane and Crabapple restaurants soon became popular places for coffee, tasty treats, business meetings, and gossip.

Home for the Arts

The Crabapple was designed with an art gallery motif, and its walls were filled with works by Northwest artists. Owner Carl Pefley, former manager of the Washington Press Club, found himself acting as an art dealer, selling paintings and then choosing replacements. Since he and his wife Pat enjoyed art shows, it was only natural that they start one of their own.

In 1947, the first Bellevue Arts & Crafts Fair was held beneath the large madrona tree in front of Pefley's restaurant. Dudley Carter's *Bird Woman* sculpture was the highlight of the fair. Carter's 12-foot *Forest Deity* had been installed as a symbol for the new mall

Above: 1946 map of downtown Bellevue. Below: Carl Pefley's Crabapple Restaurant served fine food to weary Bellevue Square shoppers

EARLY DAYS AT THE SQUARE

When Kemper Freeman Sr. developed Bellevue Square in the 1940s, the concept of an automobile-oriented shopping center was then in its infancy. Freeman traveled around the country visiting what few suburban centers there were, sometimes camping on the side of the road when no accommodation was available. He was most impressed with the Highland Park Shopping Center in Dallas and chose it as his model.

Freeman pitched his concept to Seattle architect Arrigo M. Young, who wasn't interested. Bliss Moore Jr., one of Young's junior associates, was interested. The next day Moore called Freeman and told him that he had quit the firm and wanted the job. Freeman hired him immediately.

After the mall opened, Freeman received a public relations boost from an unlikely source — Gordon Baker, Bellevue Square's barber. Baker, an Eastside resident who was approaching retirement age, had worked for years at the Olympic Hotel in Seattle, but transferred his business to Bellevue Square to shorten his commute. Many of his longtime customers began taking weekly trips to Bellevue, including William Boeing Sr. and James F. Douglas, developer of Seattle's Northgate Shopping Center. Douglas often met with Freeman to compare notes and pass along good advice.

The Square quickly became a magnet. Customers could choose from a multitude of products. Families could eat in a variety of new restaurants. Teenagers had a place to hang out and see a movie. Locals had a chance to meet, grab a cup of coffee and catch up on gossip. And Bellevue had a modern, one-stop shopping center of which it could be proud.

John L. Scott opens a Bellevue realty office in 1947, and markets Vuecrest, Bellevue's first residential development.

Lee Dennison and Ernest and Doris Van Tine plant blueberries along Mercer Slough on the future site of Overlake Blueberry Farm in 1947.

Surrey Play Barn opens with *Night Must Fall* on June 15, 1948.

A 15-year campaign to get a second floating bridge across Lake Washington begins in 1948.

earlier in the year. Some 30,000 people attended the first fair, and almost twice as many came in 1948. From that time on the numbers of attendees grew, and the Arts & Crafts Fair quickly became a Northwest tradition.

Bellevue's role in the Northwest arts scene was further bolstered in 1948 with the opening of the Surrey Play Barn, just south of downtown on 108th Avenue SE. Organized by Milo Ryan, the Play Barn produced more than four dozen plays throughout the 1950s, before development of Surrey Downs compelled the theater to move to Crossroads under a new name.

Post-War Boom

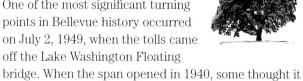

One of the most significant turning points in Bellevue history occurred on July 2, 1949, when the tolls came off the Lake Washington Floating bridge. When the span opened in 1940, some thought it would take 30 years to pay off the $5.5 million in bonds used to finance part of the construction. To the surprise of many, it took less than a decade. Miller Freeman, an early proponent of the bridge, was given the honor of paying the last nickel passenger toll.

With a free and easy commute across the lake, Kirkland was edged out as the hub of the Eastside. All roads now led to Bellevue. Kirkland held on to its ferryboats for a year, but autos could be driven directly over the new bridge to and from Seattle in less than half an hour. Hundreds of new homes were built in Bellevue, families moved in, and babies were born. Lots of babies.

A new Overlake Senior High School opened in 1949, adjacent to its War Memorial Stadium, built to

Left: Surrey Play Barn, ca. 1955. Above: The annual Bellevue Arts and Crafts Fair quickly became one of the city's most popular events. Center: Madrona tree at Bellevue Square, ca. 1946. Below: Forest Deity, ca. 1950

The American Pacific Whaling Co. goes bankrupt and whaling ships leave Meydenbauer Bay in 1948.

Overlake Senior High opens a new building in 1949.

Bill Brant opens Brant Photography in 1949.

Lacey V. Murrow floating bridge becomes toll-free on July 2, 1949.

Voters approve a $545,000 Bellevue Sewer District Comprehensive Plan on January 24, 1950.

Governor Arthur Langlie attending the floating bridge toll removal celebration, 1949

honor local heroes killed in World War II. It soon became apparent that more elementary and secondary schools would be needed to educate the children born in the baby boom. In 1950, the Overlake School District — so named in 1942 to include all the communities — was renamed the Bellevue School District now that the city was growing. Overlake High School and Elemenatry School took the name Bellevue and a site acquisition plan was developed for further school construction.

Water, Water Everywhere

By this time, Bellevue's population growth was putting a strain on its water supply. In the early days, water came from wells, but the lowering of Lake Washington in 1917 led to more than a few shortages. In 1923, the Bellevue Water Company built a tank at 96th NE and NE 8th, and in the 1930s, the firm built two more tanks on Clyde Hill.

In 1946, Water District No. 68 was formed and bought out the old company, but three years later the 1949 earthquake shifted strata, causing closure of the community's deepest well. Since water from other wells smelled funny and tasted bad, the district built a pumping station at Enatai Park in 1952 to draw and filter water from Lake Washington.

Two years later, another pumping station was built on the hill south of Meydenbauer Bay. Not only did the growing community now enjoy ample drinking water, it also could accommodate fire hydrants in case of emergencies. The days of conserving drinking water in tubs and jugs were over. Unfortunately, another problem was looming: Bellevue's sewage was being dumped into the same lake from which the population drank. Sooner or later, that dilemma too would have to be dealt with.

The Seattle Yacht Club first invites the Meydenbauer Yacht Club to join the Opening Day Parade in 1950.

The census counts 8,000 people in greater Bellevue in 1950.

The *Leschi*, the last Lake Washington ferry, takes its final run on August 31, 1950.

Overlake School District becomes Bellevue School District and receives first-class status in 1950.

Citizens, school staff, and the King County Planning Department and Commission develop a long-range plan for Bellevue schools in 1951.

An Enatai Park pumping station pumps Lake Washington water into homes beginning in 1951.

Voters defeat a ballot measure to incorporate the City of Bellevue (92 to 72) in 1951.

Voters approve an $800,000 bond issue largely to build a water filtration plant to process Lake Washington water in November 1952.

A City is Born

During the early 1950s, the community gained new schools, new housing developments, a better water supply, miles of roads, and a burgeoning business community, but no governing control to fit all these different pieces together. When voters were asked to incorporate the City of Bellevue in 1951, the provision was defeated, 92 to 72.

41

Bellevue High School students play in the snow, 1953

City boosters, led by Chamber of Commerce President Sam Boddy, spent the next two years convincing the community that local citizens were the best people to plan Bellevue's future and that incorporation was the only way to ensure this. An independent study predicted that Bellevue's growth would continue unabated, and that incorporation was the only way "to prevent a way of life from deteriorating."

The issue went back to the ballot. On March 24, 1953, voters approved incorporation by a vote of 885 to 461, and on March 31, Bellevue became a 3rd class city, with a council-manager form of government.

Eugene Boyd and Phil Reilly mark an important event in Bellevue's history.

King County Planning Commission publishes a comprehensive plan for Bellevue in its first effort to treat Bellevue as an urban center in December 1952.

Miller Freeman and A. J. Whitney sell the *Bellevue American* to Bruce Helberg and Clarence B. Laframboise on December 26, 1952.

Jane McDowell's Candies becomes the Kandy Kottage in 1952.

Citizens vote for incorporation and a council-manager form of government (885 for, 461 against) on March 24, 1953.

Clyde Hill incorporates on March 31, 1953.

Bellevue incorporates as a 3rd class city with a population of 5,940 and five-square-mile land area on March 31, 1953.

Bellevue promoters in the 1950s portrayed Bellevue as a suburban paradise

1953~1960: Gracious Living

Bellevue's first City Council elects Charles Bovee mayor on March 31, 1953.

The Council adopts the existing King County zoning plan on April 9, 1953.

The Bellevue Planning Commission holds its first meeting in the Bellevue City Club on April 15, 1953.

The Council passes Ordinance No. 8 on April 28, 1953, establishing a police department later headed by Gerald Plowman.

Bellevue's first City Council was composed of Charles Bovee, Phil Bessor, Thomas Dann, George Kardong, Melvin Love, Alden Hanson, and Albert Prince. They hired Evan E. Peterson as the first city manager and elected Charles Bovee as the first mayor. Bovee had pushed for incorporation as early as 1931, and his wife Jenny had been a prime mover in starting the Strawberry Festival in 1925.

The first council meetings were held in Bovee's home. The Veterans of Foreign Wars quickly stepped in and offered the council a room in the VFW Hall — formerly the Main Street School — at no charge save for utility fees. Although the building was infested with mice, and the women's restroom was home to a swarm of bees, it allowed the council to conduct city business over something more official than divans and coffee tables.

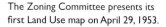

The city council's first act — Ordinance Number 1 — created a planning commission composed of Omer Mithun, Phil A. Reilly, James Littlefield, John Anderson, Joshua Vogel, Fred Herman, Frank Krepelka, W. H. Hibbard, and Phil Toman. Within the first month after incorporation, the council established an initial zoning plan, a police department, and a public works department. The Association of Washington Cities admitted Bellevue on May 1, and work continued apace on such civic endeavors as sewage disposal, a new water system, traffic control, parks, and public education.

Planning for the Future

In August, the planning commission asked Fred Herman to become the city's planning officer (later planning director). Bellevue had promise as a major city, and the commission felt that Herman was the right man to make it so. A few days later the commission hired Irving Rodley as city engineer. Herman later noted that from the start Bellevue, "was the nearest thing to a clean sheet of paper that I think any planner ever encountered."

Herman and the commission never looked at Bellevue as a small town. They insisted that the downtown core be compact, with wide streets and off-street parking provided by businesses. They zoned residential and business districts tight against each other to avoid the blight that corrodes many cities at their core. Also unusual, they required every business except gasoline service stations to landscape.

The Zoning Committee presents its first Land Use map on April 29, 1953.

The Council establishes the Department of Public Works and adopts the Bellevue Sewer District Comprehensive Plan on April 30, 1953.

The Association of Washington Cities admits the City of Bellevue on May 1, 1953.

The Council agrees to support construction of the Evergreen Point Bridge (second bridge over Lake Washington) on May 12, 1953.

The Planning Commission, guided by Joshua Vogel, recommends a Board of Adjustment on August 19, 1953.

From left to right: planning officer Fred Herman, city engineer I. S. Rodley, secretary M. N. Hos, building inspector Victor Fletcher, and assistant city engineer George Huckaby

Craig Hook riding his bike through Norwood Village, 1958

The Council establishes zoning districts for residential, business, and manufacturing on August 25, 1953.

Irving Rodley becomes City Engineer on September 1, 1953.

Enatai Elementary School opens in 1953.

Bellevue decides to use its natural creek system for open drainage instead of buried pipes on November 18, 1953.

King County transfers four street-ends to Bellevue for the first parks in 1953.

A second pumping station is installed at Meydenbauer Bay in 1953.

Bellevue creates a library board and awards the library $40 per month in 1953.

Beaux Arts incorporates as a 4th class town in 1954.

The Council elects Melvin Love as Mayor in 1954.

Some felt that the planning policies were an invasion of personal rights, and Herman was involved in more than one brouhaha over land use. At one meeting, a lawyer took a swing at him. Herman felt that citizens were very planning conscious, but had never before had the municipal machinery to work with. He later stated, "Planning was not a strange idea to them, though a lot objected to it. However, there were many responsible citizens and that made it a good place to work." The pursuit of growth, particularly through annexation, was on the agenda from the start, and prompted some adjacent neighborhoods such as Beaux Arts to incorporate in self-defense.

Porch Lights, Big City

Bellevue was grappling with the myriad challenges that come with city life, but it still maintained elements of small town charm. When Gerald Plowman was hired as police chief, his first case involved a missing donkey. During the first year, Plowman only had one police sergeant working for him, and police calls would come directly to the chief's home. If they came at night, Plowman would dispatch the patrolman by turning on his porch light.

Because Fred Herman and Irving Rodley were the only public works employees, their jobs sometimes involved smaller tasks, such as following up on citizen complaints. If a dead animal was reported on the street, the two men would flip a coin to see who would go out and pick it up. James Ditty, who didn't think much of the incorporation, ran a small newspaper and would publish photos of Herman and Rodley at work, mocking the lowly tasks being performed by "high paid city employees."

As Bellevue began changing from a rural community to a suburban one, the city made efforts to set aside land for public use, beginning a long legacy of park development. In late 1953, certain street ends were transferred from King County to become the city's first parks. These were Burrows Landing at SE 15th Street, Chesterfield Park at SE 25th Street, Clyde Beach at 92nd Street, and Meydenbauer Beach at 98th Street.

Inez Green cuts a metal ribbon with a blow torch to open the rebuilt Meydenbauer Bridge, 1950

Swimming lessons at Meydenbauer Park, ca. 1955

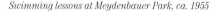

The Council establishes the Board of Adjustment with members Dale Sherrow, Hobart Stebbins, Joshua Vogel, Norman Dickerson Jr. and R. L. Elingren on January 12, 1954.

Planning Commission approves the comprehensive zoning plan on April 28, 1954.

The Council establishes the Park Board with members Gordon Wilson, Richard Carkeek, and Ralph Swenson on May 4, 1954.

The Council passes an ordinance prohibiting billboards, banners, and streamers as advertising devices on May 6, 1954.

The Council employs Wes Kennedy as City Manager on September 7, 1954.

To preserve residential areas and establish commercial and industrial districts for the projected population explosion, the Council approves the Comprehensive Street Plan and Zoning Ordinance on September 28, 1954.

The Council designates Lake Washington Boulevard as the main access to the city on October 12, 1954.

How to take care of your **Bell & Valdez Home**

SUBURBAN PARADISE

In 1955, R. H. Conner purchased 1,200 acres of farmland east of Bellevue's boundaries with the express purpose of creating an instant planned community on the model of Levittown, New York. Initially called Eastgate Hills, the subdivision would have its own infrastructure, shopping centers, parks, and 4,000 homes built by Bell and Valdez. Prices started at $13,000. It became Lake Hills.

That August, Governor Arthur Langlie (right) presided over festivities as six display homes were shown to potential buyers. The paint was still wet, and the landscape still muddy and barren, yet 45,000 prospective homeowners showed up the first weekend to see what all the fuss was about. Although some critics sneeringly referred to the subdivision as "Fake Hills," thousands of dream homes were snapped up.

Lake Hills offered all the conveniences of city life in a rural setting. Its proximity to the highway and floating bridge into Seattle was ideal for 9-to-5 commuters, many of whom were Boeing workers. The physical uniformity of the homes may have typified the suburban conformity mocked later, in the 1960s, but for some there was comfort and security knowing that the neighbors were just like you.

Lake Hills homesteaders essentially governed themselves through the Lake Hills Community Club, but by the 1960s many felt that a municipality could best handle essentials such as water, sewage, police, and fire protection. Voters approved annexation to Bellevue on the third effort in 1969, with the special concession of an independently elected Community Council that could veto any unwelcome land use plan.

The Council prohibits houseboats within the city on November 2, 1954.

Bellevue annexes the first parcels — Grocock (20 acres) and Whipple (5 acres) — on December 2, 1954.

City planners restrict building heights in the city center to 40 feet in 1954.

Thompson's Drug Store opens in Bellevue Square in 1954.

Bellevue's population is 7,658 in 1954.

Voters approve bonds to build schools and a water system in 1955.

Medina incorporates as a 3rd class city in 1955.

Hunts Point incorporates as a 4th class town in 1955.

The Lake Hills community opens with six display homes in August 1955.

Kandy Kottage candy store (formerly Jane McDowell's Candies) opens at 1910 104th NE in 1955.

Miller Freeman dies on September 18, 1955.

Bill Porter buys controlling interest in Bel-Air Chevrolet dealership in 1962.

In 1954, the council established the Park Board, made up of Gordon Wilson, Richard Carkeek, and Ralph Swenson. The same year, Melvin Love was elected mayor, and Wes Kennedy took over as City Manager. A comprehensive zoning plan and street plan were approved. Wide streets with medians and trees were envisioned, although at the time the main thoroughfare into the city was the dilapidated Lake Washington Boulevard, which crossed the south end of Mercer Slough via a rotting wooden trestle. There was much work to be done.

Original Kandy Kottage (called Jane McDowell's Candies) on Bellevue Way, 1930s

47

All-America City

Bellevue annexed its first parcels of land in 1954. The following year, the Lake Hills community opened with six display homes, and soon became the Northwest's largest planned community, with more than 4,000 homes.

In just two years since becoming a city, Bellevue's population had exploded from 5,940 to nearly 9,000. Many of these people financed their homes through Eastside Savings and Loan Association, founded by Kemper Freeman Sr. and others in 1953. It would become First Mutual Bank, the largest publicly traded financial institution headquartered on the Eastside.

Business was booming, and not just at Bellevue Square. Bill Porter became the youngest car dealer in GM history when he bought a controlling interest in the Bel-Air Chevrolet dealership at the age of 37. The little Kandy Kottage at 1910 104th NE drew lines of people around the block, satisfying many a sweet tooth. Each year new restaurants, shops, and other small businesses popped up in and around the downtown core.

Bellevue's population is 8,901 in 1955.

Bellevue celebrates its All-America City status on January 4, 1956.

The Council elects Norm Dickison Jr. as Mayor in January 1956.

Frederick & Nelson opens a remodeled branch store in Bellevue Square on August 1, 1956.

Highway 2A — the two-lane precursor to I-405 — opens in November 1956.

J.C. Penney opens in Bellevue Square in the fall of 1956.

Puget Sound Power and Light (now Puget Sound Energy) moves offices to Bellevue in 1956.

Washington Natural Gas extends gas lines to the Eastside in 1956.

Bellevue basked in the national spotlight when the January 10, 1956, issue of Look *magazine was released.*

The hard work of those who made Bellevue a successful city in such a short time did not go unnoticed. In December 1955, the National Municipal League and *Look* magazine presented Bellevue with the prestigious All America City award for citizen action that led to incorporation and for meeting the challenges that came with ensuing growth. Bellevue had achieved the attention of the nation.

All Roads Lead to Bellevue

Bellevue approves the first park bond and acquires Bellefield Nature Park and Sweyolocken Boat Launch in 1956.

The Arts and Crafts Fair becomes the "Pacific Northwest Arts and Crafts Fair" in 1956.

Bellevue's population in 1956 is 10,002.

The Library moves to the Washington State Bank building on Main Street in 1957.

Eastside Jewish residents start a Sunday School at Enatai School in 1957.

Friends of the Library form in June 1957.

In 1956, the completion of Highway 2A — the precursor to I-405 — led to more growth and development. The same year also saw the opening of a new Frederick & Nelson store at Bellevue Square, along with a second department store, J. C. Penney. Community leaders were also very proud when the region's largest private utility, Puget Sound Power and Light (now Puget Sound Energy) moved its offices from Seattle to a new four-story, $2 million headquarters on NE 4th Street. By the end of the year, the city's population passed 10,000.

In 1957, voters approved Bellevue's first park bond of $125,000, and Bellefield Nature Park and Sweyolocken Boat Launch were added to the growing list of public lands. The city grew in acreage as annexations were made. New schools were being built throughout the city, including Bellevue's second high school, Sammamish, which opened in 1959.

In 1957, the library moved from its Main Street location to the basement of the Washington State Bank Building. The new quarters were less elegant, but provided more space for books. Longtime

In 1957, the Frederick & Nelson store at Bellevue Square was remodeled

librarian Marguerite Groves supervised the move before retiring in 1958. That same year a bond issue passed for the purchase and renovation of the Sacred Heart Church on 102nd NE and Main as the library's next home.

Chace's Pancake Corral opened in 1958, and attracts a loyal following to this day. The same year Bellevue received its first major industry with the opening of Safeway's distribution center in Midlakes, and Kemper Freeman Sr. started radio station KFKF with his son. The call letters stood for the initials of both their names, but a few local wags joked that it stood for "Keep Feeding Kemper Freeman."

49

The Freemans entertain their friends, 1960

URBAN PARADIGM

In 1955, the City of Bellevue was only two years old, and already had a firm grasp on many issues involved in running a municipality. Schools, traffic, water supplies, sewage systems, police protection, zoning, urban planning, and park development were some of the many challenges Bellevue had already confronted in the face of unprecedented growth.

Beginning in 1949, the National Municipal League handed out awards each year to cities deemed most All-America. Sam Boddy Jr. and Bill Brant, co-chairs of the Bellevue Chamber of Commerce publicity committee, saw an opportunity to promote the good work being done in Bellevue. They sent an entry to *Look* magazine, co-sponsor of the competition, detailing why Bellevue signified all that is American.

Out of 137 municipalities, Bellevue was one of 11 chosen to win the coveted award. On January 4, 1956, schools were let out and a parade was held downtown. That evening, Bellevue celebrated with a banquet at Bellevue High School auditorium, where two students were chosen as All-America boy and girl. Governor Arthur Langlie presented certificates to 35 community leaders before the major award was presented in the spotlight. Afterwards, fireworks lighted the skies over downtown Bellevue.

The award proved helpful in promoting the city to potential homebuyers and merchants.. The following year, the Chamber of Commerce published a guidebook to Bellevue's businesses, neighborhoods, and community groups. Nearly every page was emblazoned with the award, along with the enticing invitation to experience "gracious living."

★ ★ ★
ALL AMERICA CITY
AWARD WINNER
BELLEVUE
WASHINGTON

Ground was broken for Overlake Hospital in October 1959 (Gunderson)

To Your Health

The decade ended with the opening of Overlake Hospital, a dream of Bellevue residents that began in 1953 when Ann Seeger, Lorraine Weltzien, and a group of their neighbors on Clyde Hill formed Fabiola, the first hospital auxiliary. All of these women had small children, and were concerned that the closest hospitals were in Kirkland and Seattle. Any traffic snarl or bridge closure could mean the difference between life and death.

The women raised money through door-to-door campaigns, raffles, "Hospitalities" stage shows at the Playbarn, and even a grudge golf match between James Ditty and Kemper Freeman Sr. The auxiliary also started the annual "Bandage Ball," which still raises money every year. The auxiliary's goal was to found a hospital that was not-for-profit, non-sectarian, and open to everyone.

The national Hill Burton Act allocated money to build hospitals in growing areas, as long as the community owned the land and came up with 60 percent of the construction costs. Land was sought first in the Lake Hills neighborhood, but supporter Don McCausland came up with the idea of local merchants and physicians buying up property near the NE 8th interchange at Highway 2-A, which provided easy access by automobile. The land would then be given to the hospital.

The community rallied and ground was broken in October 1959. The hospital was scheduled to open at 3:00, October 16, 1960, but an early arrival led to a change of plans. Mrs. Rose Cziprian had gone into labor that morning, and was taken to the hospital at 10:13. Only an engineer and housekeeper were in the building, but thankfully Gloria McNeill, director of nurses, showed up and was able to call in the obstetrician. At 11:04, Katherine Mary Cziprian was born, just in time for that afternoon's festivities.

The Council elects Kenneth Cole as Mayor in 1958.

Safeway builds a distribution center, Bellevue's first big industry, in Midlakes in 1958.

Voters defeat the first METRO Plan, including sewage disposal, rapid transit, and metropolitan planning, on March 11, 1958.

Chace's Pancake Corral on Bellevue Way opens in 1958.

Kemper Freeman Sr. starts KFKF radio station in 1958.

Voters create the METRO sewer utility that begins cleanup of Lake Washington in September 1958.

Voters pass a bond issue to purchase and renovate the Sacred Heart Church on 102nd NE and Main for the Bellevue Library in September 1958.

First Mutual Bank

Founded by Kemper Freeman Sr. and other local business people on January 17, 1953, First Mutual Bank has grown from its beginnings in a 10 x 20-foot room in Bellevue Square to become the largest publicly traded financial institution headquartered on the Eastside.

Knowing that money for mortgage financing would be critical to the region's future, Freeman tried to convince numerous Seattle banks to open branches in Bellevue. When they did not, he decided to form his own. Named Eastside Savings & Loan Association, the bank's original mission was to provide mortgage loans for families wanting to buy homes on the growing Eastside.

The bank changed its name to First Mutual Savings Bank in 1968 when it became a member of the Federal Deposit Insurance Corporation (FDIC). It was converted to a publicly traded institution in 1985 and changed its name once again to simply First Mutual Bank. Around the same time, First Mutual expanded from primarily single-family residential lending into commercial real estate lending. The bank also began to offer checking accounts in addition to savings products.

In the early 1990s, First Mutual began moving in some new directions and developed the additional services of a full-service community bank. This included expanding the income property lending division, adding consumer loans and lines of credit, creating an innovative national sales finance division, and placing greater emphasis on small-to-mid-size-business banking. A custom construction lending department was also developed and expansion continues on the banking center system.

Bellevue's population is 11,250 in 1958.

Yarrow Point incorporates as a 4th class town in 1959.

The *Bellevue American* chooses a woman — Helen Bucey — as "Man of the Year" in 1959.

Bellevue's second high school, Sammamish, opens in 1959.

Bellevue installs its first traffic light at Main Street and Bellevue Way in 1959.

Bellevue's population is 12,100 in 1959.

The City Council elects Jim Buck as Mayor in 1960.

The *Bellevue American* renames "Man of the Year" to "Outstanding Citizen" and honors Jane Wood in 1960.

The P-X supermarket burns down in 1960.

Overlake Memorial Hospital opens on October 16, 1960.

Sherwood Forest Elementary, Robinswood Elementary, and Tyee Junior High (now Middle School) open in 1960.

Bellevue's population is 12,800 in 1960.

1961~1970: Bridge Work

John Danz Theatre on 106th NE

L. Joe Miller is hired as the new city manager on January 4, 1961.

The Sacred Heart Church building reopens on January 6, 1961 as the Bellevue Public Library. Mrs. Nanon Hilburn Jones serves as librarian. The library has about 20,000 books at this time.

Siegfried Semrau, recent German immigrant, is hired as Parks Director on February 20, 1961.

The Crossroads Shopping Center opens in 1961 at 156th NE and NE 8th.

American Wholesale Grocery moves into its $1.2 million distribution center in 1961.

Washington Natural Gas establishes an eastern division in 1961 at 156th Avenue NE and NE 8th Street.

United Control opens a $2 million electronics plant in Overlake Park in 1961.

Temple Sinai is founded in 1961.

By the mid-1950s, it was apparent that one bridge across Lake Washington was inadequate to serve the burgeoning Eastside population. Various plans were discussed, including a second bridge adjacent to the existing Mercer Island floating bridge, a span from Sand Point to Juanita, and even a tunnel underneath the lake.

Squabbles over cost and design led to many delays. The final location for the bridge was between Montlake and Evergreen Point, and it was hoped that the new span would be open in time for the 1962 World's Fair in Seattle. Construction began in 1960, but the bridge didn't open until August 28, 1963.

Governor Albert Rosellini, who had made a campaign promise that the bridge would be completed under his watch, cut the ribbon on opening day. The $34 million construction project was a boon for the Eastside, especially for Bellevue, which was now situated between two bridges. Just as the first span opened up Bellevue for development, so the second solidified the young city's future growth and progress. The construction of I-405 commenced soon after the second bridge was complete and further cemented Bellevue's role as the Eastside hub.

This signpost used to welcome visitors at Bellevue Way and 108th NE.

Not Your Average Joe

Another major influence on Bellevue's future was L. Joe Miller, hired in 1961 as city manager, a job he held for the next 16 years. Miller became the catalyst for

Welcome to Beautiful **BELLEVUE**

GREATER BELLEVUE CHAMBER OF COMMERCE — 339-104TH N.E. GL 4-2464

KIWANIS CLUB THUR. NOON VILLAGE·INN

JUNIOR CHAMBER OF COMMERCE — 1ST THUR. NITE WEATHERVANE

ROTARY CLUB TUES. NOON CRABAPPLE

LIONS CLUB WED. NOON WEATHERVANE

ALTRUSA 1ST AND 3RD THUR LINCOLN FIRST FED.

V.F.W. POST 2995 1ST AND 3RD MON 8PM V.F.W. HALL

B'NAI B'RITH LODGE 2040 — 3RD THUR. 8-30
B'NAI B'RITH CHAPTER 917 — 4TH THURS. 8-30

EXCHANGE CLUB WED. NOON CRABAPPLE

BUSINESS & PROFESSIONAL WOMEN'S CLUB

Bellevue's expansion by means of annexations. Miller was also a leader in establishing the city's infrastructure from fire protection services, to arterial construction, to emergency response, to environmental stewardship.

As the city grew, so did the small towns around it. To fend off concerns that it might be annexed, Clyde Hill incorporated mere hours before Bellevue did. Beaux Arts incorporated in 1954, followed by Medina and Hunts Point in 1955, and Yarrow Point in 1959. These towns occupy the area west of north Bellevue.

Fred Herman (left) discusses plans for Bellevue's future, 1970. Below: Bellevue Public Works director Robert McCormick at the opening of the Evergreen Point floating bridge (City of Bellevue)

Miller led the way to annexing land to the north, west, and south. During this time, Bellevue's downtown started growing up, not out. The first "tall" building in the business core was the four-story Puget Sound Power and Light Building, which opened in 1956. In 1967, the seven-story 400 Building became Bellevue's first "skyscraper." From that point forward, downtown Bellevue began looking more like a city, with high-rise construction that continues to this day.

Before the city began rising skyward, one of Miller's first tasks was to implement downtown "superblocks," which were separated by six-lane arterials and two- and four-lane secondary streets. Local Improvement District (LID) taxes were assessed on adjacent properties to pay for the construction, and every street in downtown Bellevue was rebuilt, starting with 104th Avenue, now Bellevue Way.

As the city expanded, more businesses chose to locate in Bellevue. In 1961,

The 104th Avenue Local Improvement District (LID) iis completed in 1962 from NE 8th to NE 12th Streets. Six lanes, drainage, curbs, sidewalks, streetlights, and trees are added. Overhead power and phone lines are moved to back alley positions, since underground lines were not feasible at the time.

The John Danz Theatre opens in 1961 at 600 106th Avenue NE.

Plugging into Bellevue

In December 1956, Puget Sound Power & Light Company formally opened its new Bellevue headquarters, from which it has evolved into today's Puget Sound Energy. The company, best known simply as "Puget Power," can trace its roots back to the demonstration of Seattle's first electric light bulb in 1886, and it built a regional empire providing electric utility and rail transportation services from Bellingham to Tacoma by World War I.

Competition from municipally owned utilities and tightening state and federal regulations led Puget Power to refocus on serving metropolitan Puget Sound's growing suburbs after World War II – hence its decision to become the first major regional corporation to pick Bellevue for its business address. Over the next 50 years, Puget Sound Power & Light acquired more than 150 companies and transformed itself into one of the largest private utilities in the country, responsible for power production, transmission and delivery to 1.4 million customers.

Bellevue resident John Ellis led much of this expansion as the company's CEO between 1976 and 1993, when he "retired" to organize and direct local ownership of the Seattle Mariners baseball club. Puget Sound Power & Light merged with the state's largest natural gas distributor, Washington Energy, to form Puget Sound Energy in 1997.

Bellevue's population in 1961 is 13,100.

The City Council elects Scott McDermott as Mayor in 1962.

Bellevue Way (Then 104th Avenue) is widened in 1962 from NE 8th to NE 13th streets.

Area voters approve a $575,000 levy in 1962 to establish a junior college.

The Parks and Recreation Department establishes the first citywide recreation program in 1962.

American Wholesale Grocery opened a $1.2 million distribution center in Midlakes, and United Control opened a $2 million electronics plant in Overlake Park. Downtown, the curtains were raised on the John Danz Theatre, a magnet for movie buffs of all ages. Crossroads Mall opened. And throughout the city, small mini-mall shopping centers began dotting the landscape.

Sieg Semrau

Up until the 1960s, Bellevue's only parks were Meydenbauer Bay, which had been developed as a WPA project in the 1930s; Clyde Beach; and various small street-end parks. In 1961, Siegfried Semrau was hired as Parks Director. The growing city was practically a blank slate for the enthusiastic landscape architect.

Semrau, a German, was captured during World War II and sent to England, where he worked as a prisoner on a number of large English estates. After the war, he made his way to the states, and ended up in Bremerton. When Bellevue hired him as Parks Director, Fred Herman helped him study for his citizenship examination.

Semrau was instrumental in acquiring and creating Bovee Park, Bellefield Nature Park, Hidden Valley Sports Park, Enatai Park, Kelsey Creek Park, and many others. He also led the way in the creation of the Bellevue Municipal Golf Course. Semrau's promotion of parks and public spaces was so convincing that the public passed bond issue after bond issue in favor of land acquisition and development.

Sieg Semrau (left) inspects the green at Bellevue Municipal Golf Course (COB)

Civic Pride

Bellevue had a growing sense of civic pride from all that had been accomplished during its first seven years as a city, but its City Hall left much to be desired. In 1960, the municipal staff moved out of the old VFW Hall into a building on 106th Avenue. At the time, city staff numbered around 60 people, and the new space was overcrowded from the start.

Even though city workers were thrilled not to share office space with bees and mice, as they had in the old building, a new city hall was needed – one that would match the progressive and professional tone being set by city leaders. Various locations were considered until property was finally selected at the corner of Main Street and 116th Avenue SE – land that was first settled by Clark Sturtevant nearly a century ago.

L. Joe Miller, who became the catalyst for Bellevue's expansion

Some worried that the new building was located too far from downtown, but it was decided that Bellevue was a city of cars, and that

President John F. Kennedy recognizes Bellevue High School teacher Elmon S. Ousley as National Teacher of the Year on April 22, 1963.

Albert Rosellini cuts the ribbon on August 28, 1963, to open the Albert D. Rosellini Memorial Evergreen Point Floating Bridge — the second Lake Washington floating bridge.

Interstate 405 construction begins in 1963.

Bellevue School District purchases 70 acres for the junior college in 1963.

Bellevue's population in 1963 is 14,057.

The City Council elects Clarence Wilde as Mayor in 1964.

Newport High School is completed and opened in 1964.

Aerial view of City Hall and the Bellevue Library, ca. 1965. Below: Grand opening of Bellevue City Hall, March 7, 1964 (COB)

The new Bellevue City Hall at Main Street and 116th Avenue SE is dedicated on March 7, 1964.

The Westminster Chapel, a non-denominational church, is founded in 1964.

The 104th Avenue NE interchange on State Route 520 opens in 1964.

people drove where they needed to go, including to City Hall. An adjacent overpass was built over I-405 – formerly known as Highway 2A — and the new City Hall was formally dedicated on March 7, 1964. The police department was located in the basement. The Bellevue Fire Department was organized the next year.

A Cultured Community

In 1965, ground was broken next door to city hall for the new library. It opened in 1967. Its most striking feature was a stucco lustro mural by Viennese artist Sepp Mayrhuber, who donated the artwork in memory of his mother-in-law Marguerite Groves, the city's first librarian. The seven-by-ten-foot mural represented the library as a link between past and present.

By this time, Bellevue had a thriving arts community. The Pacific Northwest Arts and Crafts Fair continued to grow in popularity, so much so that the Pacific Northwest Arts and Crafts Foundation formed as a non-profit, fundraising arm of the PNW Arts & Crafts Association. In 1967, the Bellevue Philharmonic orchestra was founded, as was the Bellevue Film Festival.

Also in 1967, the Bellevue Play Barn Children's Theater raised its curtains at the Center Stage Theater at Crossroads Shopping Mall. Founded by Ralph Rosinbum and Louis Lotorto under the auspices of the Bellevue Play Barn, the Children's Theater presented a variety of plays during the summer months from 1967 to 1977. The first production was *The Adventures of Tom Sawyer*, starring Eastsiders Richard Dorrish and John Harsh.

The Sepp Mayrhuber mural was moved from the old library to the current building. Below: Dale Chihuly blows glass at the Arts & Crafts Fair, 1968 (BAM)

Higher Education

As the leading edge of the post-war "baby boom" reached its teens, more secondary schools were built to accommodate them. Sammamish High School opened in 1959, followed by Newport High School in 1964, and Interlake High School in 1967. The number of elementary schools in the Bellevue School District continued to increase.

Virginia Detwiler organizes the first Town Hall lecture series in 1964. The series brings in celebrity speakers and is one of the only big shows in the Puget Sound area at the time.

Bellevue's population in 1964 is 14,250.

The sewage treatment plant at 102nd Avenue SE and SE 6th Street is abandoned in 1965 and the new Metro pumping station is activated, eliminating discharge into Lake Washington.

The City of Bellevue purchases Fire Station One from King County in 1965 and organizes the Bellevue Fire Department.

Pacific Northwest Arts and Crafts Foundation is formed in 1965 as a nonprofit fundraising arm of the PNW Arts & Crafts Association.

A $1,500,000 park bond is approved in 1965. Hidden Valley Sports Park and Chism Beach Park are acquired.

Bellevue's population in 1965 is 18,900.

In 1962, voters approved a $575,000 levy to establish a junior college. On January 3, 1966, Bellevue Community College (BCC) opened with some 450 students and 40 faculty members. Classes were held in portable buildings on the campus of Newport High School until the fall of 1969, when the new campus was completed at its present location near Eastgate.

58

BCC led the way in embracing the cultural changes that were sweeping the country. In 1966, the college offered a class on Negroes in History, and later held workshops in black awareness, women's studies, and minority affairs.

Children's Theater production of The Reluctant Dragon, *1968. Below: Construction of the PACCAR Building (COB)*

Ten Times the City

In 1969, Bellevue annexed Lake Hills, and began eying unincorporated land farther north where a new shopping center was being built. The city also welcomed two community councils, East Bellevue and Sammamish – the second and third such councils in the state — which have veto power over land use issues within their boundaries. Voters abolished the Sammamish Community Council in 2002.

Downtown, the 13-story Business Center Building opened on NE 8th, making it the tallest building in the city at that time. Pacific Car & Foundry moved its corporate offices from Renton into the new skyscraper, which would

PACCAR Inc

Founded in 1905 as Seattle Car Manufacturing by William Pigott, the company initially built railcars and trucks for the growing Northwest logging industry. In 1917, Seattle Car became Pacific Car & Foundry, and produced hundreds of tanks and military vehicles during World War II. The company changed its name to PACCAR Inc in 1972 and is now guided by Chairman and CEO Mark Pigott, great-grandson of the company founder.

PACCAR moved its corporate headquarters from Renton to downtown Bellevue in 1969. The company initially occupied two and a half floors of the Business Center Building, at the time Bellevue's tallest high-rise. Today PACCAR is the largest Fortune 500 company with headquarters in Bellevue and occupies the entire PACCAR Building.

PACCAR has become a global technology leader in the design, manufacture and customer support of high-quality light-, medium- and heavy-duty trucks bearing the Kenworth, Peterbilt, DAF, and Foden nameplates. Kenworth and Peterbilt have earned top rankings for customer satisfaction. DAF trucks have been consistently recognized for their quality and durability throughout Western Europe and the United Kingdom. PACCAR also manufactures and markets Braden, Carco, and Gearmatic industrial winches.

PACCAR's operating success has made it the world's most profitable truck company. It has earned positive net income since 1939 and has paid a dividend every year since 1941. PACCAR is positioned to maintain the profitable growth its shareholders expect by delivering quality products and services that have made the company a leader in the markets it serves worldwide.

PACCAR supports a wide variety of community endeavors. Through the PACCAR Foundation – established in 1951 – the company has contributed more than $35 million to local civic, health, and educational organizations that serve Bellevue and the region. Major beneficiaries include Overlake Hospital Foundation, Bellevue Community College, Bellevue Downtown Park, and Bellevue agencies that provide specialized care for early childhood development, mental health, and elder health care. PACCAR is a major sponsor of this book and other 50Fest projects and events.

Bellevue

60

come to be called the PACCAR Building as the company grew to occupy every floor.

Also that year, the Holiday Inn Motel and Convention Center opened as Bellevue set its sights on becoming not only a regional center of commerce, but also an international one. The city welcomed a delegation from Yao, Japan – the first of four sister cities around the world.

When the 1970 census was tallied, 61,196 Bellevue residents appeared on the rolls. This was five times the number counted in 1960, and a whopping tenfold change since incorporation. In less than two decades, Bellevue had gone from a little town on Lake Washington to the fourth largest city in the state.

Pacific Coca-Cola Bottling Company begins building a plant in 1967 at 124th and Bel-Red Road.

The Lake Hills Library opens in 1967.

Bellevue's population in 1967 is 29,500.

The 13-story Business Center (now PACCAR) Building on NE 8th and 106th NE opens in 1967.

The City Council elects Kenneth Cole as Mayor in 1967.

The Fisher Farm is purchased in 1968 to become Kelsey Creek Park. It also serves as the temporary headquarters of the Bellevue Parks Department.

Mayor Ohashi of Yao, Japan, leads an official delegation to Bellevue in 1968 for the formal signing of the sister city proclamation.

M. Frank Odle retires in 1968 after a 55-year educational career in Washington, 50 of which were in Bellevue.

Bellevue Community College. Below: Protest march on Bellevue Way

DONALD PHELPS — TRAILBLAZER

Donald Phelps was born in 1929, the grandson of John T. Gayton, one of Seattle's black pioneers. In 1960, Phelps began his teaching career at Robinswood Elementary School as a teacher of fourth, fifth, and sixth grade students. In 1963, he was appointed principal, becoming the first black principal in the Bellevue School District. Four years later, he was named principal of Bellevue Junior High School, where he instituted the first flexible class scheduling and the first computer assignments. He was the first black secondary school principal in the state.

Phelps resigned from this position in 1969 to protest racism, but continued to support the district's voluntary integration program. After a stint as a news commentator for KOMO TV and Radio — where he spoke regularly on race relations — he returned to education as interim superintendent of the Lake Washington School District. From there, he moved upward to become president, then chancellor, of Seattle Community College, before moving to Los Angeles, where he became chancellor of Los Angeles Community College District, the nation's largest community college system.

Before his death in 2003, Phelps taught in the community-college leadership program at the University of Texas. Throughout his career, he committed himself to hiring women and minorities. He often served as consultant and speaker to many organizations across the country, and had many honors bestowed upon him.

East Bellevue Community Council, the first Bellevue community council, and the second in the state, is formed in 1969.

The Holiday Inn Motel and Convention Center opens in 1969 on Main Street and 112th Avenue SE.

Bellevue annexes Lake Hills on March 10, 1969.

The 1,500-acre Sammamish Annexation is added to the city on November 4, 1969. The Sammamish Community Council is Bellevue's second community council.

Classes start at Bellevue Community College in the fall of 1969.

The City Council elects Kenneth Gates as Mayor in 1969.

The annexation of many housing developments and communities results in a 1970 population of 61,196, making Bellevue the fourth largest city in the state.

Cherry Crest Elementary opens in 1970.

Borghild Ringdall Middle School opens in 1970.

The Tally building on 112th Avenue NE opens in 1970.

A 1970 Mercer Slough study by engineers, botanists, biologists, and the State Fisheries Department shows it is dying from siltation and off-season flooding from development. A canal system is proposed.

Tollgates for the Evergreen Point floating bridge, ca 1975. Top right: The bridge today (COB)

1971~1980:
Growth and Responsibility

As it became a large city, Bellevue had to deal with regional issues more so than many small towns. In the early 1970s, massive layoffs at Boeing affected the entire Puget Sound region. The "Boeing Bust" hit hard in Bellevue, home to many aerospace workers. In 1972, the Employment Opportunities Center opened to help laid-off Boeing employees find work. Once the local economy bounced back, the nonprofit group expanded to assist immigrants with job training, education, and citizenship programs.

Bellevue also found itself at the center of regional transportation issues. A study done in 1968 called for a new highway — Interstate 605 — to be built east of and parallel to I-405 to prevent congestion on the Eastside as well as in south King County. Regional planners felt this was a more palatable solution than double-decking I-405. Nearly 1,000 Bellevue families showed up at a hearing to protest the new highway, and even when the proposed route was moved east of Lake Sammamish, strong opposition continued.

Eventually, the plans were abandoned. Controversy had arisen in the early 1970s when it was reported that proponents of I-605 owned property near the route. Soon afterwards, another study indicated that the highway wasn't needed at all. Even though I-605 was never built, it did lead to the widening of 148th NE (I-605's original alignment), giving Bellevue a principal arterial with high aesthetic standards. At the same time, Bellevue became one of the first cities in King County to erect barriers to protect neighborhoods from traffic noise.

Bellevue Fire Department cigarette patrol car, ca. 1975. Below: The Bellevue Police Department often sent out whimsical cards like this during the Christmas holidays. Inset: Police Chief Donald Van Blaricom

Help Is On the Way

A big city with big city problems needs emergency and police services. The Bellevue Fire Department was created in 1965, although paid firefighters staffed the station only during the day. Until 1980, volunteers were still on call after hours. Beginning in 1969, Bellevue absorbed all of Fire District No. 14, which included Medina, Beaux Arts, Hunts Point, Yarrow Point, and Clyde Hill. Taxpayers in these communities reimbursed Bellevue for emergency services.

After Bellevue residents learned in the 1960s that fire trucks carried medical equipment and oxygen to treat injured firefighters, calls for emergency medical assistance began to climb. The department treated first aid calls as a low priority at first, but the public embraced the new service. After Seattle instituted Medic One in 1970, Bellevue citizens passed the hat to raise several hundred thousand dollars for their own Medic One, which began responding to calls on September 5, 1972. Within three years, the number of medical calls exceeded the number of fire calls.

Ground is broken for Eastgate Plaza in 1972.

The Seattle Trust building (10655 NE 4th Street) opens in 1972.

The Summit Ridge building (108th Avenue and 104th Street) opens in 1972.

Medic One begins Eastside service on September 5, 1972.

Bellevue's population in 1972 is 62,343.

Water Districts 68, 97, and 99 are merged in March 1973, to operate as the City of Bellevue's Public Utilities Department.

KELSEY CREEK PARK

In 1921, the W. H. Duey family leased and cleared the land that is now Kelsey Creek Park. The Dueys built a large barn and started Twin Valley Dairy. They delivered bottled milk and home-churned butter, and their son Fernley became Bellevue's first veterinarian.

In 1944, Ray and Nettie Fisher took over the farm, phased out the dairy operation, and raised beef cattle. They continued to operate it until 1969, when they sold 79 acres of it to the city. The Bellevue Parks Department used the house on the property as headquarters as they turned the farm into what many consider Bellevue's most popular park, named after H. E. Kelsey, a schoolteacher who moved to Bellevue in 1884.

The Parks Department took great effort to preserve the rural atmosphere of the park by continuing to operate a working farm so that children can see barnyard animals like the late, beloved donkey Pasado (right) up close. Large fenced pastures hold cattle, horses, goats, sheep, and pigs. Chickens, rabbits, and smaller animals are also housed in the buildings, and recreational programs are given in animal care and farm experience.

The park also features the Fraser cabin (above), one of Bellevue's surviving pioneer structures. Originally built in 1888 at the corner of what is now NE 7th Street and 127th Avenue NE, the cabin was moved to Kelsey Creek Park in 1974 after Brooks Johnston donated it to the city in 1966.

In 1975, Police Chief Donald Van Blaricom took over the duties from Chief Nick Giardina, who had served since 1959. Both men saw the city grow dramatically, and both aggressively modernized the department. Bellevue installed high-visibility blue emergency lights on the patrol cars before any other department in the state. Bellevue was also one of the first cities to train its officers in how to handle domestic violence cases. And although the city's crime rate was low, Bellevue detectives were able to act quickly on high-profile cases, such as the 1973 Bellevue Sniper incident, a highway shooting spree that left one dead and one injured.

One innovation that did not bear fruit was the proposal by City Manager L. Joe Miller in the 1970s to create the position of Public Safety Officer. Miller proposed that police officers, firefighters, and paramedics could be cross-trained in each other's jobs to save money. Police could respond to fire department calls and idle firefighters could serve in police roles. The affected departments successfully argued against these multiple duties, but a legacy of this idea survives in the fact that Bellevue police supervisors are Lieutenants like their counterparts in the fire department, instead of the more conventional police department rank of Sergeant.

Who Will Stop The Rain?

Bellevue's rapid growth led to a closer examination of environmental issues. Bellevue had built its own sewage treatment plant years before Metro began cleaning up Lake Washington in the 1960s, and over the years care was taken to keep Bellevue and the surrounding countryside as clean and green as possible. In 1974, the city was one of the first in the nation to implement a storm and surface water utility and to retain

The Downtown Development Board is incorporated on June 24, 1974. Board Members: Jeff Holland — Exec. Dir., James Gilleland, Kemper Freeman Sr., Kay Wilson, Frederic Danz, Ken Greenbaum, Harold Leitz, Joe Lynch, Paul Vander Hoek, and Bob Wing.

Plans for the expansion of Bellevue Square into a north-south oriented, two-level enclosed mall are announced in 1974.

A managed creek bed in Bellevue, ca. 1980 (COB)

ALL ACCORDING TO PLAN

Bellevue has always had a planning vision," according to Matt Terry, the city's planning and community development director since 1983, "but there has always been tension over the question of what kind of city Bellevue should be." This debate came to a head in 1973 and 1974 as the city debated a new comprehensive plan to guide its evolution from semi-rural to suburban, and, ultimately, urban.

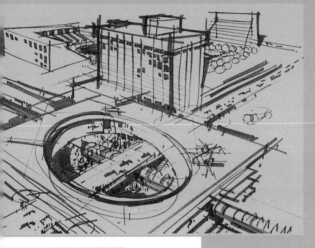

Chris Smith Towne was a newly elected member of the Bellevue City Council as it grappled with the simultaneous challenges of a new storm water utility, sign controls, parks development, and a new comprehensive plan to make sense of two decades of, in her words, "relentless annexation." The 1974 plan affirmed seemingly contradictory goals, she recalls: "Preserve Bellevue's suburban single-family residential quality and create a local economy that could generate a job for every qualified resident."

The 1974 plan's emphasis on residential values triggered a reaction from business people who feared that their economic needs would be neglected. A business plan for a denser downtown in turn alarmed neighborhood leaders such as Maria Cain. Working with the new Bellevue Downtown Development Board (BDDB, later Bellevue Downtown Association) and Bellevue City Council member Nancy Rising (pictured above), a "wedding cake" scheme was devised to step down densities from the downtown core to its fringes. A 1978 amendment adopted this new thrust for downtown and formalized a dozen other planning "subareas" for residential neighborhoods. This strategy established a model plan for all of Washington with adoption of the state's Growth Management Act in 1990.

The East King County Convention and Visitors Bureau opens in 1974.

Bellevue's population in 1974 is 63,940.

The Bellevue Art Museum opens in the Chapel of Flowers on the SE corner of the Bellevue Square block in 1975.

The *Journal American* newspaper is founded on August 17, 1976, combining the *Eastside Journal* and the *Bellevue American*, both acquired by Longview Publishing Company headed by John McClelland Jr.

The City Council elects Milford Frank "Mel" Vanik as mayor in 1976.

Bellevue's population in 1976 is 67,000.

L. Joe Miller resigns and Dick Cushing becomes acting City Manager in 1977.

Bellevue Parks Director Lee Springgate at Bellevue Botanical Garden (Photo by Kurt Smit, Seattle Post-Intelligencer*)*

rather than bury or divert its numerous streams, using them instead of sewers to channel runoff and reduce flooding. The City charged property owners utility fees based on how much of their land was covered with impervious surfaces such as buildings and parking lots.

A storm drainage utility based on property fees was not without its detractors. Some people felt they were being charged for rain, and that rain was free. Because of delays, Boulder, Colorado, became the first city in the nation to implement such a utility, although Bellevue's model was chosen by many cities throughout the United States.

Work on the surface water utility also led to the protection of more than 50 miles of open streams throughout the city. Years later, when the federal government listed Puget Sound salmon as an endangered species, Bellevue was in a better position to respond than most cities. In addition, the utility is closely involved with the protection of wetlands and with the restoration of wildlife habitats.

Main Street is remodeled from 104th to 100th through a Local Improvement District (LID) financed by 50% local merchants' and 50% City funds.

A $4,750,000 Park Bond is approved in 1977.

The Bellevue Library has the second highest circulation in the state in 1977. Lynn Lancaster becomes the third librarian in its 54 year history.

Bellevue's population in 1977 is 68,500.

The City Council elects Gary Zimmerman as Mayor and William Parness is appointed City Manager in 1978.

Lee Springgate is named the Bellevue Parks Director in 1978. He began as an intern in the City Manager's Office in 1970, and moved three months later to a position in the Parks Department.

Green's Chapel of Flowers, ca. 1979

Leisure Time

Bellevue's Parks Department led the way in ensuring that residents had an abundance of natural landscape and open space to enjoy. Parks Director Siegfried Semrau was instrumental in the creation of Kelsey Creek Park, Enatai Beach, and the Municipal Golf Course. Lee Springgate, his successor after 1978, more than doubled the amount of park space during his 21-year tenure. He concentrated on a "pearls on a string" approach to park management, whereby public lands are connected by proximity and trails.

The "One Percent for Art" fund is adopted for city art projects in 1978.

The Land Use Code is adopted, replacing the old zoning code, in 1978.

The Floodplain Code is adopted in 1978, limiting building in flood-prone areas and allowing Bellevue to participate in the federal flood insurance program.

The Old National Bank Plaza building (10800 NE 8th Street) is opens 1978.

Bellevue's population in 1978 is 72,700.

Bellevue Junior High, the former Union S High School, closes in 1979.

Bill Gates with Microsoft Executives in Bellevue and old Microsoft campus on Northup Way, ca. June 1983 (© Doug Wilson/CORBIS). Next page: Bellevue Square before remodeling, 1979

In the 1970s cultural awareness continued to grow. The Bellevue Arts Commission was formed in 1975, the same year the Bellevue Art Museum opened in Green's Chapel of Flowers on the corner of Bellevue Way and NE 4th. In 1978, Bellevue established a One Percent for Art fund for public art projects.

Bellevue citizens were well read. In 1977, the Bellevue library had the second highest circulation in the state. The city had a strong newspaper, the daily *Journal American*, formed by the merger of two weeklies, the *Eastside Journal* (founded in Kirkland in 1918) and the *Bellevue American* (founded in 1930), under the guidance of publisher John McClelland Jr. and editor Frank Wetzel.

Further Developments

Even with the economic downturn in the early 1970s, Bellevue continued to be a magnet for business and industry as well as for new residents. The City adopted a new comprehensive plan to preserve the character of its neighborhoods while involving the Bellevue

Downtown Development Board to "plan and promote development to achieve a quality environment for people living and working in Bellevue." Thanks to a pioneering policy of downtown "densification," more buildings began to rise downtown, many of them bank offices. The BDDB was also instrumental in implementing the "wedding cake" layout of downtown buildings, with smaller buildings at the perimeter and taller buildings towards the center.

Other areas of the city saw new business development as well. In 1973, the $3 million Eastside Medical Center opened in Overlake Park. That same year, Eastgate Plaza opened. A few years later, the northern tip of Mercer Slough was dredged to create an office park, and in 1979 Factoria Mall opened.

Bill Parness resigns as City Manager and Dick Saunders, Finance Director, is appointed acting City Manager in 1979.

The City of Bellevue purchases the Overlake Blueberry Farm in 1979.

Tolls are removed from the Evergreen Point Floating Bridge on June 22, 1979. Kemper Freeman Sr. pays the final toll, just as his father had done on the original floating bridge.

Bellevue's population in 1979 is 77,515.

Plans to build the Evergreen East shopping center are dropped in 1980 after four years of legal battles with Kemper Freeman Sr., the City of Bellevue, and King County.

Ground-breaking ceremonies are held for the new Bellevue Square on February 29, 1980. It will become a $142 million redevelopment.

Andrea Beatty is appointed City Manager in 1980, and is the first woman to manage a city as large as Bellevue anywhere in the United States.

Kemper Freeman Jr. and Sr. break ground for Bellevue Square's remodel

BELLEVUE SQUARE
GROUND BREAKING
FEB. 29, 1980

In 1978, a tiny software company moved from Albuquerque, New Mexico, to a bank building in downtown Bellevue. Within two years, business was so good that they moved to a much larger office complex along Northup Way. In the early 1980s, the company's young founders, Bill Gates and Paul Allen, moved their headquarters just over the city line to Redmond, but Microsoft continues to significantly influence Bellevue's economy, as well as its traffic congestion.

A Tale of Two Malls

The Public Safety Bond is passed in 1980, financing a new communications center, training center, and new fire stations.

The Honeywell building (600 108th Avenue NE) opens in 1980.

The United Olympic Life building (110 110th Avenue NE) opens in 1980.

Eastside Catholic High School opens in 1980 across from Bellevue Square in the former Junior High school.

Harriet and Calhoun Shorts donate their home and seven and a half acres of land in 1980 to the city for a park. Located at 12001 Main Street, it later becomes the Bellevue Botanical Garden and the centerpiece of the 106-acre Wilburton Hill Park.

Church of Jesus Christ of Latter-day Saints temple is dedicated at 2808 148th SE on November 17, 1980.

Bellevue's population in 1980 is 73,903.

In the mid-1970s, developer Bert McNae undertook plans to build an industrial and shopping park, called Evergreen East, in the Overlake Park and Evergreen Highlands communities, just over the city boundary in Redmond. Kemper Freeman Sr. opposed the project, feeling that two major shopping centers in such close proximity could not survive. City officials agreed, and became concerned that Bellevue Square — the heart of their tax base — would suffer.

The City brought lawsuits, and legal battles went on for years. During this time Freeman took the opportunity to plan and promote the expansion of Bellevue Square. Evergreen East plans were dropped in 1980, and because the public opposed an outward expansion of the Square, Kemper Sr. and his son Kemper Jr. began plans to convert it into a multi-level mall.

Groundbreaking at the new Bellevue Square took place on February 29, 1980. Kemper Sr. used a shovel and Kemper Jr. used a bulldozer to illustrate the difference between two generations. Phase one of the project opened in 1981 to much success, and was the precursor to even more changes downtown. The Evergreen East site became home to the Microsoft campus, ironically, just outside Bellevue city limits.

SEAL OF APPROVAL

For 25 years, a harbor seal named Butch was friend and neighbor to many folks living along Lake Sammamish. He was first seen in the lake in 1950, most likely abandoned by someone who tired of him as a pet. Nearby homeowners were at first befuddled by the ocean mammal's appearance in fresh water, but many became amused by Butch's antics, and took a shine to him. Bellevue Mayor Nan Campbell, who moved next to Lake Sammamish with her family in 1952, fondly recalls how her children grew up on a first-name basis with a harbor seal.

Whether Butch was popping up out of the water to splash people on docks, gliding up under swimming dogs to tug on their legs, or just sunning himself on the shore, the lake's star attraction was a source of delight to many. Occasionally, Butch would run afoul of someone who didn't like having a seal in the neighborhood, and Fisheries officers would be called in. Butch eluded the lawmen every time, sometimes with a little help from his friends.

In his later years, the aging seal became aggressive. In the summer of 1975, he chased two little girls out of the water, and even dragged a dog off a dock. The Washington State Department of Game intervened, and captured Butch with nets. The plan was to provide the seal with medical treatment and release him into Puget Sound, but Butch passed away while in captivity. At the time of his death it was noted that Butch lived long past the normal span for his kind, due to his lack of natural enemies and an abundance of caring friends in the lake community.

The Mercer Slough in the 1980s (COB). Below: Bellevue Art Museum exhibit in its former Bellevue Square gallery (BAM)

1981~1990: Square Roots

Kemper Freeman Sr. died in 1982, but not before witnessing the first phase of Bellevue Square's transformation from a one-level, open-air shopping center to a multi-level, enclosed mall. Besides increasing capacity to accomodate nearly 200 businesses, the Square also saw expansion of its three department stores — Nordstrom, Frederick & Nelson, and J. C. Penney. In 1984, the Bon Marché became the mall's fourth retail anchor.

Although shoppers welcomed the changes to Bellevue Square, some longtime Bellevue residents were saddened to see the loss of popular mall fixtures such as the nearby Chapel of Flowers, which had

hosted many marriages and memorial services over the years. In its last years before demolition, it housed the Bellevue Art Museum, later relocated to the top floor of the expanded mall.

Also gone was the old Bel-Vue Theatre, and with it, the annual Bellevue Film Festival. But the largest concern was over the potential loss of much of the landscaping surrounding the Square. In response, developers saved and relocated many of the trees, and planted more than 700 new trees around the property.

Both the Bellevue Airport and the infamous floating bridge "bulge" disappeared in the 1980s

Wheels Keep On Turning

Expansion of the mall brought more traffic, and multi-level garages were built for 3,800 cars. Meanwhile, growth outside the Square continued apace. More skyscrapers appeared downtown, and more hotels opened along I-405 and elsewhere. Once a bedroom community for Seattle, Bellevue became a place to travel to, as well as from.

Bridge traffic gave evidence of this. In the 1950s and 1960s, morning commuters drove mainly west, to Seattle, and evening commuters drove east, back to their homes. In the 1970s, the phrase "reverse commute" came into vogue when it became apparent that just as many people were commuting from Seattle to the Eastside as were going the opposite direction. Early state

plans to expand I-90 to perhaps 18 cross-lake lanes provoked opposition from neighborhoods and environmental lawsuits from Seattle, Mercer Island, and the Eastside.

The project was delayed for a decade while cities and community groups negotiated environmental mitigations such

The Red Lion Hotel opens in January 1982.

The City Council elects Roy Ferguson as Mayor in 1982.

Kemper Freeman Sr. dies on October 20, 1982.

The Bellevue Art Museum opens on the third level of the new Bellevue Square on January 30, 1983.

Bellevue Airfield closes on May 2, 1983.

The 24-story Skyline Tower Building (10900 NE 4th) opens in 1983.

The 21-story One Bellevue Center building (411 108th NE) opens in 1983.

The 16-story Plaza Center Building (10900 NE 8th) opens 1983.

The first annual Peter Puget Festival is held from July 22-24, 1983.

Hualien, Taiwan, becomes Bellevue's second sister city in 1983.

as lids in Seattle's Central area and on Mercer Island. Work resumed in 1981 to replace the East Channel Bridge to Mercer Island and to eliminate the floating bridge "bulge" opening that had once given large ships access to the south end of Lake Washington. By the end of the decade, construction began on a new floating bridge parallel to the first. On November 25, 1990, most of the original floating bridge, which was under repair, sank during a violent storm. Another was built to replace it.

Changing Times

The City of Bellevue and its citizens continued to cope with the rapid changes brought by progress. In 1981, the Bellevue Downtown Association, the Bellevue City Council, and the Bellevue Chamber of Commerce spearheaded passage of the Downtown rezone. It limited buildings to 300 feet or 25 stories, and allowed them to be built closer together. This strategy concentrated new office, retail, and financial activities in the downtown corridor, saving residential neighborhoods from development pressure. The downtown plan was unique among suburban communities, most of which tended to have sprawling areas of office concentration instead of Bellevue's compact layout.

Great steps were also taken to expand and develop more park land. In 1984, two of three parks bonds passed, totaling more than $10 million. The third proposition to build a downtown park at the site of the old high school and elementary school failed by a narrow margin,

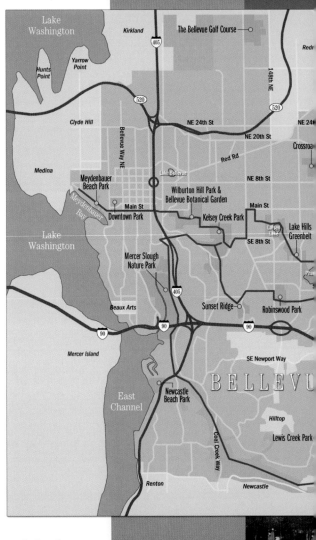

Major City Parks

Other Parks

City Limits

City Trails

DOWNTOWN PARK

In 1984, voters passed two of three propositions in a landmark Parks Bond. Prop. No. 1 earmarked $5.065 million for improvements to parks and recreational areas and Prop. No. 3 allocated $5.095 million for public safety and improvements to roads, walkways, and trails linking Bellevue parks. Prop. No. 2, which requested $2.09 million for the partial development of the Downtown Park, failed by a few score votes.

The Bellevue School District, original owner of the 17-acre site, sold it to the city of Bellevue in 1984 for $15 million — one of the largest single municipal land purchases in state history. City officials, led by Mayor Cary Bozeman, hoped to develop it into a large park to stimulate multi-family residential development around it.

The vote devastated Bozeman, but he and the city organized a private nonprofit group to develop the first phase of the park. Led by John Ellis and Carol James, the Downtown Park Citizens Committee raised $1.8 million in private contributions from major employers such as Puget Power, and in 1988 campaigned successfully for the passage of a second bond issue.

Beckley/Myers Architects of Milwaukee, Wisconsin, won a national competition for the design of the park. Phase one opened in 1987, and the pedestrian promenade and canal were unveiled in 1990 as part of the completed Phase II.

Downtown Park

Lake
amamish

Park

Issaquah

The Society for the Preservation of the Old Bellevue Community (the future Bellevue Historical Society) is founded in 1983.

Bellevue's population is 79,500 in 1983.

The City Council elects Cary Bozeman as mayor in 1984.

The Bon Marché store opens in 1984 during the final phase of Bellevue Square's redevelopment.

In 1984, the Bellevue School District sells the 17-acre downtown park site to the City of Bellevue for $15,000,621 for a downtown park. The Union S School building, Bellevue Junior High, and Bellevue Elementary were all located on this site.

Voters pass Propositions 1 and 3 of the 1984 Park Bond.

Citizens form the Downtown Park Committee after Proposition 2's failure in 1984.

Bellevue's population is 78,620 in 1984.

Andrea Beatty resigns as City Manager in 1985 and Phillip Kushlan replaces her.

Lake Heights Elementary closes in 1985.

The Bellevue Elementary school building is torn down in 1985 to make way for the first phase of the Downtown Park.

FUTURE
DOWNTOWN
PARK SITE   City of Bellevue

I-90 and I-405 interchange under construction.

but a citizens' committee stepped in and raised $1.8 million in corporate and private donations to build it anyway.

During the 1980s and 1990s, much of Bellevue's transformation into a "city in a park" was due to the efforts of Parks Director Lee Springgate, an advocate of park development philosophies put forth a century earlier by Frederick Law Olmsted. Springgate believed that parks were more than just recreation centers, that they should be valued as ecological resources and as meditative, even spiritual spaces.

Backed by city government and Bellevue's citizenry, Springgate worked to connect many of Bellevue's parks by trails, providing a path of nature and greenery between Lake Washington and Lake Sammamish. In some cases, bond issues were passed to acquire and "bank" park land for later development as more funds became available.

A City for Everyone

By the 1980s, the city had progressed from a small town to a major city. The question now was whether to focus on remaining a suburban home for families or to become a major economic and employment center. Some envied Bellevue's upscale image and others felt it was a symbol of bland suburban life. Both misinterpreted the city's maturation into a distinctive and diverse urban community.

For years, white middle-class families constituted the predominant populations of Bellevue and the Eastside, but in the 1980s, the same things that had drawn earlier families to Bellevue — safe neighborhoods, good schools,

All junior highs (grades 7-9) change to middle schools (grades 6-8) in 1985.

Fire Station No. 7 opens (SE 8th) in March 1985, bringing some 90% of the Bellevue Fire Department service area within a five-minute response time for fire suppression and Medic One calls.

The Bel-Kirk Drive-In closes in 1985.

Bellevue's Metro Transit Center opens in 1985 at NE 6th and 108th NE.

Construction starts in 1985 on the first high-rise residential building in Bellevue, the Penny Farthing Project at 108th NE.

Voters annex the Bellevue Library into the King County Library system on May 21, 1985.

Bellevue Historical Society members hold first meeting at the home of Margot Blacker on October 5, 1985.

Bellevue's population is 80,250 in 1985.

Preserving the Past

In the 1980s, as more and more construction and development occurred throughout the city, some residents felt that much of Bellevue's past was being lost or was in danger of being forgotten. In 1985, the Bellevue Historical Society was founded to protect, preserve, and create awareness of the city's heritage. Founders held their first meeting at the home of future City Council Member Margot Blacker.

One of the organization's first projects was reviving the annual Strawberry Festival, which had been suspended during World War II when Japanese farmers and their families were relocated to internment camps. Since its founding, the society has recorded oral histories from these Japanese American families as well as from scores of other longtime residents representing all walks of life.

In the late 1980s, BHS members convinced the city to save the historic Winters House, located on Bellevue Way near the Mercer Slough. Although in disrepair, the building was restored to much of its former glory, and became home to the historical society's collection of photographs, artifacts, and historical documents. In 1992, the Winters House was listed on the National Register of Historic Places

In 2001, the Bellevue Historical Society, under the stewardship of director Karen Klett, merged with Redmond's Marymoor Museum to become the Eastside Heritage Center. The following year King County abruptly evicted the Marymoor collection from its longtime home. EHC is now exploring options for a new museum and heritage center in or near downtown Bellevue.

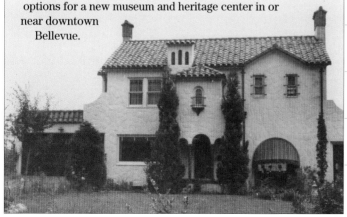

The Pacific First Plaza building (155 108th NE) opens in 1986.

The Rainier Bank Plaza building (NE 8th and 108th NE) opens in 1986.

First annual Bellevue Downtown Association's Festival of Music held in July 1986.

The City Council votes unanimously in 1986 to partner with the King County Library system to buy the 6.9-acre Ashwood School on NE 12th — closed in 1978 due to low enrollment — for the new Bellevue Regional Library site.

John McClelland Jr., president of Longview Publishing Co., sells the *Bellevue Journal American*, the *Mercer Island Reporter*, and the *Port Angeles Daily* to The Persis Corp. of Hawaii in 1986.

Bellevue Downtown Association holds the first annual "Art Grazing" event in January 1987.

The 17-story Pacific Regent Building, a high-rise retirement community, opens in 1987.

Phase one of the Koll Center building (500 108th NE) opens in 1987.

Phase I of the Bellevue Downtown Park opens on September 13, 1987.

The Bellevue Historical Society revives the Strawberry Festival in 1987.

The first portion of the 6th Street pedestrian corridor opens downtown in 1987.

Bellevue's first woman Mayor, Nan Campbell (shown in 2003) and first woman City Manager, Andrea Beatty (1980)

and strong local businesses — now began drawing people from a broader array of cultures. By 2000, census counts showed that more than one-fourth of Bellevue's population was born outside the United States, and its schools served one of the state's largest populations of students for whom English was not their first language.

Women became a driving force in the city as they became more active in business, politics, and service organizations. In 1980, Andrea Beatty was appointed City Manager — the first woman in the nation to manage a city as large as Bellevue. In 1988, Nan Campbell became the first woman to serve as mayor of Bellevue. A longtime resident, Campbell was a dedicated advocate of social services and improvements for the West Lake Sammamish and Crossroads communities. Campbell also was an early champion of Bellevue's surface water utility, which established an innovative storm drainage system to reduce flooding, and better prepared the city to respond to endangered salmon listings in the late 1990s.

Construction begins in 1987 on the largest single-phase commercial project, Bellevue Place, which planned 800,000 feet of office, retail, and hotel constructed around exterior and interior public open space.

Some 300 citizens attend the city's first annual "Open House" in September 1987.

Ringdall Middle School closes in 1987.

Bellevue's population is 82,070 in 1987.

The City Council elects Nan Campbell as mayor in 1988.

The first phase of Bellevue Place (10400 NE 8th) opens in 1988, including the Hyatt Regency Hotel and the 21-story Seafirst Bank Tower.

The Lakes Club opens on top of the Security Pacific Plaza in 1988.

In 1988, *Architecture* magazine selects Bellevue, Baltimore, and Charleston, SC as up-and-coming U.S. cities with the most progressive architectural designs.

Voters approve a $16.5 million park bond issue on September 20, 1988, $3 million of which is earmarked for completion of the Bellevue Downtown Park.

For the first time in 20 years, voters approve a $67 million library bond issue for the King County Library System in 1988.

Crossroads' Resurrection

By the mid-1980s, the Crossroads Shopping Center was rapidly deteriorating. Built in 1962 with the ambition of competing with downtown Bellevue, the mall and its immediate neighborhood attracted alienated youth and petty criminals.

Metro Director Neil Peterson and Bellevue Mayor Gary Zimmerman kick off the "Bel-Hop" shuttle bus.

In 1986, San Francisco-based Terranomics took over the center, and managing partner Ron Sher stepped in to reconnect the shopping center with the local community. Rather than luring customers away from Bellevue Square, Sher realized that the center's strength was its community value as a "third place" — a social nexus and modern agora between work and home for Crossroads residents.

79

Sher attracted new tenants that better fit the needs of neighbors, such as a grocery store, barber shops, restaurants, movie theaters, bookstores, and travel agencies, and created a welcoming food court serving foods as diverse as the residents of Crossroads. City officials joined the effort by establishing the nearby Crossroads Community Center, which offers youth and family services, as well as arts and recreation classes. Crossroads Shopping Center also houses a mini-City Hall and a community police station.

Bellevue City Council approves a $100,000 a year annual budget for public art in 1988.

The 11th Annual Jazz Festival moves from Bellevue Community College to Downtown Park in 1988.

Bellevue's population is 85,180 in 1988.

Bellevue Junior High and the former Bellevue High buildings are torn down in 1989 to make way for Downtown Park.

Voters reject the proposed annexation of Eastgate in 1989.

Bellevue Art Museum holds a $200,000 Frank Lloyd Wright Exhibit in October 1989.

Bellevue begins a curbside recycling program in 1989.

Enrollment at Bellevue schools drops from 24,000 in 1969 to 14,000 in 1989. Although the population has grown, family sizes have not.

Bellevue's population is 86,350 in 1989.

The City Council elects Terry Lukens as mayor in 1990.

The City Council levies a per employee "head tax" on businesses to pay for street improvements in 1990.

Phase II of Downtown Park opens in September 1990.

Sections of the Lacey V. Murrow Bridge sink on November 25, 1990.

Bellevue's population is 86,874 in 1990.

The soaring economy of the 1990s triggered construction of new office towers, condominiums, and cultural facilities such as the Bellevue Art Museum (upper right), while the city protected open spaces such as Phantom Lake (Gunderson)

No traffic fatalities are reported in 1991, the first time since 1972.

City police begin bike patrols in 1991.

City raises downtown building height cap to 450 feet.

The Washington State Summer Games are held in Bellevue, Issaquah, Redmond, and Kirkland in August 1991.

Bellevue's population reaches 87,898 in 1991.

The Frederick Winters House is placed on the National Register of Historic Places on April 21, 1992.

Mayor Cary Bozeman and City Manager Phil Kushlan appoint 16-member Cultural Diversity Task Force in 1992.

1991~2004: Boom Town

Bellevue's progress was significant in the 1980s, but the burgeoning high tech industry brought unprecedented prosperity to the city in the 1990s and solidified Bellevue's status as an independent economic center both on the Eastside and in the Puget Sound area. Although Microsoft moved its corporate head-quarters to Redmond, related software companies developed in Bellevue. In 2003, the city had an estimated 18.4 percent of King County's high-tech-jobs, and more than ten percent of all jobs in the county. It houses the headquarters of such

cutting edge companies as PACCAR, Western Wireless, Expedia.com, Esterline Technologies, Drugstore.com, Coinstar, and several leading software developers.

In the mid- to late 1990s, construction cranes became a familiar sight on the city's skyline as the tech boom cre-

ated extraordinary demand for office space. Height limitations on buildings were raised from 300 to 450 feet. By the turn of the new century, new office and residential buildings created a significant skyline for the downtown. Also during the 1990s, the number of residential units in downtown Bellevue quadrupled, and the city added a new library, art museum, and convention center.

The State Growth Management Act, which limited the spread of urban growth into rural areas and encouraged delivery of urban services by cities rather than by counties, helped to accelerate the city's annexation of unincorporated neighborhoods surrounding it. Between 1990 and 2003, property owners in Newport Hills, Lake

Frederick & Nelson chain goes out of business in 1992.

Metro adds 60,000 hours of bus service to the Eastside in 1992.

Liepaja, Latvia, becomes the third sister city to Bellevue in December 1992.

Bellevue's population reaches 88,580 in 1992.

Regional "Inaugural Day Storm" damages the Evergreen Point Floating Bridge on January 20, 1993.

Bellevue annexes the "Garden of Eden," land bordered by I-405, 120th SE, and SE 60th and 64th streets on February 16, 1993.

Seattle looms in the distance from Bellevue's Somerset neighborhood. Below: Bellevue Branch of the King County Library System (Gunderson)

Heights, Factoria, Enatai, Lakemont-Newcastle, and West Lake Sammamish decided to join the City of Bellevue. In most cases they chose to annex to the city to take advantage of its services and low taxes made possible by the city's strong mix of business and residential properties.

Since its incorporation, Bellevue always looked to a future when it would be known not as a suburb of Seattle, but as a full-fledged city in its own right. This goal became policy in 1996, when the Bellevue City Council voted unanimously to drop out of the Suburban Cities Association, an advisory group of 37 municipalities in King County. Since then, Bellevue has increasingly played a leadership role in the planning and management of regional services and facilities such as jails, courts, freeways, high-capacity transit, and water supply.

The bursting of the "Dot.com bubble" and the post-September 11, 2001, economic slump in the early 21st century deflated more than a few Bellevue high-tech start-ups and delayed construction of the new Lincoln Center project, but Bellevue endured. While the state, King County and other cities had to

At the urging of the Bellevue Historical Society, the City dedicates cherry trees in Bellevue's Downtown Park to commemorate the many contributions of Bellevue's Japanese American community, on May 19, 1993.

Government Access channel 28 airs first televised Bellevue City Council meeting on June 1, 1993.

The Bellevue Library at 11501 Main closes its doors on June 18, 1993, and the new Bellevue Regional Library opens at 1111 110th Avenue NE on July 1, 1993.

The new I-90 bridge is dedicated as the Homer M. Hadley Memorial Bridge, honoring the original floating bridge's engineer, on July 17, 1993.

Bellevue annexes the South Newport II neighborhood, adding 195 acres and 1,780 people to the city on July 26, 1993. This neighborhood is bordered by SE 64th, and SE 69th streets, 112th Avenue SE and 128th Avenue SE.

slash budgets to survive, protecting the solvency of Bellevue's already efficient city government required relatively modest adjustments. Bellevue's half-century commitment to practical growth management, progressive government, and prudent taxation was put to the test by a deep national — and deeper regional — recession.

BELLEVUE'S SISTER CITIES

In 1956, President Dwight D. Eisenhower proposed a program for American cities to affiliate with those of other nations in the spirit of international friendship and cooperation. The nonprofit Sister Cities International now includes 3,500 cities in 138 countries worldwide.

In 1969, Yao, Japan, became Bellevue's first sister city. A group of Yao dignitaries later attended the dedication of the oriental gardens at Kelsey Creek Park, now at the Bellevue Botanical Garden. Over the years, delegations from both cities have crossed the Pacific for ceremonies, conferences, and special city functions.

Hualien, Taiwan, became Bellevue's second sister city in 1984, followed by Leipaja, Latvia, in 1992, and Kladno, Czech Republic, in 1993. Each has participated in student exchanges, official visits, and other community projects. On March 31, 2003, as part of Bellevue's 50Fest celebration, delegates from all four cities met together in Bellevue for the first time in the city's history.

The first Eastside Community Street Fair takes place at Robinswood Park in 1993.

The $73 million replacement Lacey V. Murrow Bridge opens on September 12, 1993.

The new Meydenbauer Center convention facility, with a 36,000 sq. ft. exhibition hall, opens at NE 6th Street and 112th Avenue SE on September 20, 1993.

Chinese-born Conrad Lee becomes Bellevue's first non-white City Council member with his election on November 2, 1993.

Bellevue City Council votes 5-2 to annex Factoria on December 13, 1993.

Kladno, Czech Republic, becomes Bellevue's fourth sister city in 1993.

Bellevue's population in 1993 is 89,710.

The City Council elects Don Davidson as Mayor in 1994.

Restored Winters House opens on May 10, 1994.

The John Danz Theatre closes on August 5, 1994, with final running of the film *Forrest Gump*.

The City Council halves garbage taxes in 1994, and votes to forego the usual 6% increase in property-tax collections.

A new police precinct opens in Factoria Mall on September 28, 1994.

A mini-City Hall opens in the Crossroads Shopping Center on October 31, 1994.

Controversial "bikini strip club" called Babe's Cabaret opens in Factoria on December 8, 1994. It soon closes due to neighborhood protests.

Although many commuters leave their cars at home thanks to facilities such as Metro's Bellevue Transit Center, I-405 remains one of the state's busiest highways (Gunderson)

Highways and Byways

Transportation issues continued to be an ongoing challenge as the city, county, and state grappled with the task of keeping Eastside traffic flowing as smoothly as possible. Bellevue's downtown transit center opened in the mid-1980s, and in 1992, more than 60,000 hours of bus time was added to the Eastside. Ten years later, Metro expanded the transit center to 12 bays. Eastside voters rejected the initial Sound Transit plan in 1995, which would have provided light rail service across Lake Washington, but a downscaled regional plan won passage in 1996. Rail transit has long divided the Eastside, facing stiff opposition from Kemper Freeman Sr. and his son, while supported by others.

Major changes were made to I-90 and SR-520, especially at their interchanges with I-405, which were also expanded and modified. The new I-90 bridge, named for Engineer

Bellevue-based QFC Food Stores (Quality Food Centers, Inc.) buys out Olsen's food Stores, Inc. in a $58 million deal on December 27, 1994.

Bellevue's population is 99,140 in 1994.

Bellevue-based Lamonts Apparel Inc. files for bankruptcy on January 6, 1995.

HILLTOP

Hilltop, one of the Bellevue area's most distinctive neighborhoods, is actually not part of Bellevue. In fact, annexations have embraced all of the land surrounding the community, making Hilltop an island unto itself. In some ways, this is what those who formed the community in 1947 might have intended.

During the postwar building boom of that time, architects Perry Johanson, John Morse, and Fred Bassetti weren't interested in the for-profit developments that were sprouting up in the suburbs of Seattle, and instead decided to form a nonprofit venture that would create a residential collective of other like-minded individuals. They purchased 60 acres of land on the hill above Factoria and subdivided it into 40 one-acre lots, with twenty acres left over for common land and roads.

Eighteen families chipped in up to $150 apiece to have a well dug, and these people — many of whom were professors at the University of Washington — are considered to be Hilltop's founders. Such notable architects as Paul Hayden Kirk and Wendell Lovett built homes in the "modern" style, as called for by the community's prospectus. A greenbelt surrounds the community as a buffer against the encroaching suburban landscape, and is cared for in a collaborative effort amongst residents.

Over the years, Hilltop has received high praise in many housing and architectural publications. When the first houses were built in Hilltop, it was the only community on the hill. Now surrounded by Bellevue, there are some who believe that Hilltop will some day join the city, although many community members still enjoy their autonomy.

A strip club opens at 2239 148th Avenue NE in the former Papagayo's nightclub to angry citizen protests on January 25, 1995.

City Hall activates its electronic online bulletin board (a primitive Website) on February 27, 1995.

King, Pierce, and Snohomish county voters reject a $6.7 billion regional "Sound Transit" bus and rail plan in March, 1995. Sixty % of Eastsiders vote no. This opposition also helps stall plans to impose tolls on stretches of SR 520 and 522.

Bellevue's Town Hall lecture series closes with its 30th season on April 24, 1995.

Papagayo's nightclub shuts down on May 30, 1995.

"Use it Wisely" campaign begins in June, 1995 urging citizens to carpool, use public transit, and cut down on car trips.

Bellevue Place and the Bellevue Hyatt Hotel (HistoryLink). Below:
Children play in the Factoria Mall (Gunderson)

Homer Hadley, opened in 1993, parallel to the rebuilt Lacey V. Murrow Bridge. Discussions began on upgrading the SR-520 bridge, which was starting to show its age after 40 years.

Bellevue's major arterials also received a facelift, expanding access into and out of downtown. Soon after the start of the new century, work began on the I-405 overpasses, including NE 8th and NE 4th. A new off-ramp was built south of Main, connecting I-405 with 116th SE. Major improvements were made to Richards Road, Factoria Boulevard, and 140th NE, and the aging Meydenbauer Bridge on Lake Washington Boulevard was replaced.

Protect and Serve

By 2003, emergency medical services accounted for 70 percent of Bellevue Fire Department's responses. Four medical units, each staffed by two paramedics (with nine months of intensive training each and supervised by a physician) provided 24-hour coverage from Lake Washington to Snoqualmie Pass.

Unhindered by the restraints of routine and tradition that dominate older agencies, the Bellevue Fire Department also embraced a culture of innovation. As the city grew from suburban to urban, the department looked ahead to meet the challenge of high-rise buildings and high-density housing. In 1994, the department organized

Steve Bauer is named City Manager on July 3, 1995, replacing Phil Kushlan who left in February 1995 after 10 years in the position.

Fire Station No. 8 opens at 5701 Lakemont Blvd. on July 8, 1995.

Washington Mutual Plaza at 106th Ave and NE 2nd Street opens on July 19, 1995.

The Bellevue Pacific Tower office-condominium opens in 1995.

Bellevue's population climbs to 102,000 in 1995.

The City Council elects 29-year-old Ron Smith as mayor in 1996.

Bellevue City Council votes unanimously to leave the Suburban Cities Association, an advisory group of 37 municipalities in King County, on February 16, 1996.

The *Journal American* becomes the *Eastside Journal* on November 16, 1996.

The Meydenbauer Bay Marina roof collapses under snow and ice, crushing 40 boats, on December 29, 1996.

The landmark Wilburton trestle provides a scenic route for the "Spirit of Washington Dinner Train" (Gunderson)

a Light Force, consisting of a pumper truck and a ladder truck paired as a single unit to respond to emergencies in high-density areas. A second Light Force was added in 2002.

Major crime has been rare in Bellevue. No murders occurred in the city between 1998 and 2003. In earlier years, Bellevue police investigated such high-profile cases as the George Russell murders, which involved a "signature killer" who took the lives of three women in 1990, and then posed their bodies to mark the crime. Two years later, when the popular donkey Pasado was brutally slain in Kelsey Creek Park, Bellevue police lifted latent fingerprints from a piece of wood — a remarkable accomplishment — to identify the animal's teenage killers. Pasado's death sparked state legislation to increase the penalties for animal cruelty.

Bellevue's population rises to 103,700 in 1996.

Bellevue's worst murder occurs in 1997 when all four members of the William Wilson family are killed by two neighborhood youths.

The City Council votes 4-2 in 1997 for an ordinance requiring group homes to undergo a four-month review by neighbors and city officials before opening.

The City Council approves $100,000 in 1997 for "Bellevue Beyond 2000," a program suggested by City Manager Steve Bauer to chart a better future for Bellevue's community.

The Shorts' historic cabin and their
more modern home remain in use
in the Bellevue Botanical Garden

A Rose by
Any Other Name

As Bellevue annexed more land, parks were added to serve the city's new neighborhoods. But in the heart of Bellevue, near the old community of Wilburton, a unique park took seed and grew into one of Bellevue's most popular destinations.

In 1984, Calhoun and Harriet Shorts deeded their home and seven acres of gardens to Bellevue. Five years later, the Bellevue City Council set aside 17 acres for the botanical garden, including the Shorts property. Another 19 acres south of the garden were set aside as a botanical reserve.

Beginning in the early 1990s, the Shorts' residence was converted to a visitor center, and the grounds were landscaped to include a 1.2 mile trail throughout the gardens, which were tended by the Bellevue Botanical Garden Society and the Northwest Perennial Alliance. Kelsey Creek's Yao Garden, named for Bellevue's Japanese sister city, was relocated to the site, and new beds were added

EDUCATION EXCELLENCE

The cover of the February 2, 2003, edition of *Newsweek* magazine featured Bellevue High School student Jasmin Hagen for its rating of America's top 100 high schools, of which Bellevue was home to five. Bellevue, International, and Newport high schools were in the top 20, and Sammamish and Interlake also made the honor roll. These prestigious rankings are indicative of the effort Bellevue has put into public education for more than a century.

Bellevue's first bond issue in 1892 funded the construction of a two-room schoolhouse at the corner of Main and 100th NE. The building served the community well for many years. Long after Bellevue students had moved into newer and more modern school buildings, the old Main Street School became the community's first City Hall when Bellevue incorporated in 1953.

One of Bellevue's most notable educators was M. Frank Odle, who has the distinction of holding the longest teaching career in state history. Odle began teaching in Snohomish County in 1913, and came to Bellevue in 1918 as superintendent of the old Bellevue School District No. 49. After local school districts consolidated in 1942, Odle returned to full-time teaching — everything from science and history to girls basketball — until his retirement in 1968.

In recent years, Bellevue schools have kept up with changes in classroom demographics. Between 1969 and 1989, school enrollment dropped from 24,000 to 14,000 due to smaller family sizes within the district.

In the 1990s, the student population underwent a noticeable change in diversity. The number of Asian students increased by 26 percent and the number of Hispanic students increased by a factor of three. In 2003, the district began offering Spanish immersion studies, in which English-speaking students begin at kindergarten to receive almost all of their subject matter instruction in Spanish.

The City Council halts new permits for adult-entertainment establishments in Bellevue in June 1998.

The City Council votes unanimously on December 13, 1998, to annex Enatai, an affluent 43-acre neighborhood with 296 residents that lies just north of I-90 on Lake Washington.

Bellevue's population is 105,700 in 1998.

Lee Springgate, Bellevue Parks Director, retires in November, 1999, after 21 years in the position. Patrick Foran becomes the third Parks Director in the city's history.

The Bellevue Galleria retail complex opens in 1999.

Bellevue's population rises to 106,200 in 1999, but thanks to annexations, Vancouver passes Bellevue to becomes the state's fourth largest city.

The 22-story KeyCenter office building opens in 2000.

Due to the efforts of the Bellevue High School class of 2000, the road leading to the school is renamed from Kilmarnock to Wolverine Way.

1953-2003

90

to include fuchsias, dahlias, rhododendrons, and many other flowers. The Bellevue Botanical Garden opened in 1992, and has been growing ever since. The park's wintertime Garden d'Lights display, in which flowers are created with mini-lights, is now an annual favorite.

Bellevue 50Fest

As Bellevue approached the half-century milestone in its journey as a city, the Eastside Heritage Center invited public officials, business and community leaders, and citizen volunteers to plan a year-long commemoration of the community's history and accomplishments. Scores of organizations and individuals responded and organized a variety of projects and events for what became known as Bellevue 50Fest.

The celebration was kicked off on March 31, 2003 — the 50th anniversary of Bellevue's incorporation — with a party at Meydenbauer Center. Hundreds listened to speeches, munched birthday cake, and witnessed a re-enactment of the crossing out of the "un" on Bellevue's "unincorporated" sign, an event staged by Phil Reilly and Eugene Boyd for newspapers 50 years earlier. Reilly had passed on to higher real estate, but Boyd's grandson Brad Kirkpatrick was there with Reilly's son, Brian, to repeat the historic vandalism before a cheering audience.

Bellevue's 50Fest observance followed a "retro" theme with its logotype, poster, exhibits, and events such as the "Bellevue Motorama" and "Dance As You Were" sock hop and hula hoop contest (HistoryLink)

During the year, 50Fest organized a 1950s-style Sock Hop, an Arbor Day planting of 50 trees — including several Giant Sequoias — along the Lake Hills Connector, a time capsule photo contest, a Motorama car show, and 71 neighborhood celebrations. A new portable historical exhibit was displayed at these events as well as at shopping centers and other gathering places. The city produced an historical video and the *King County Journal* published a multi-week "History Hunt" contest whose ultimate winner, Marie Matthews, was flown along with her husband Frank, as VIPs to Hualien and Yao, Bellevue's sister cities in Taiwan and Japan.

50Fest culminated on March 31, 2004, with the sealing of a 50-year time capsule and the publication of the book you hold in your hands. The rest is the future.

Bellevue Historical Society and Marymoor Museum officially merge to form Eastside Heritage Center on March 12, 2001.

Lincoln Square, a $360 million project across the street from Bellevue Square, begins construction in 2001.

The City Council unanimously votes on December 10, 2001, to purchase two-thirds of an acre on Meydenbauer Bay from former City Councilman Bill Lagen, grandson of William Schupp, owner of American Pacific Whaling Company.

By 2001, Chicago developer Sam Zell, chairman of Equity Office Properties Trust, owns 50% of the total office space available in downtown, valued at $493 million, including Rainier Plaza, City Center Bellevue, One Bellevue Center, and KeyCenter, all acquired in the past four years. Kemper Freeman Jr.'s holdings amount to $245 million.

Eastside office vacancy rate rises from 2% to 10% in 2001, following the dot-com bust. It eventually rises to 28% before starting to recover in 2003.

Bellevue's population is 111,500 in 2001.

The City Council elects Connie Marshall as Mayor in 2002.

The newly expanded Bellevue Transit Center (BTC) reopens with 12 bays in 2002.

Voters approve bonds totaling $324 million in 2002 to rebuild 21 schools.

The City Council declines a voter-approved $645,000 property-tax levy in 2002 to maintain parks because voters had twice rejected an accompanying bond measure to buy more park land.

The City Council approves purchase of the Qwest Communications building at 450 110th Avenue NE for $29 million on November 25, 2002, to serve as new police and fire department headquarters and a new City Hall.

Famous Sons and Daughters of Bellevue

The following is an incomplete list of celebrities and notable citizens who were either born in Bellevue or have called the city their home for a significant time:

ANN & NANCY WILSON — Graduates of Sammamish and Interlake High Schools respectively, who went on to form the Rock and Roll band Heart.

JEFF PROBST — 1979 graduate of Newport High and host of televison's *Survivor* series.

ANN REINKING — 1967 graduate of Bellevue High School. Got her start dancing in Bob Fosse musicals in the 1970s, and is now considered the leading acolyte of Fosse's style and technique.

JOHN ELLIS — Puget Power CEO and Seattle Mariners CEO.

ALVIN M. "TEX" JOHNSTON — Boeing test pilot best known for his aileron roll of the Boeing Dash-80 over Lake Washington at the 1955 Seafair celebration.

WILLIAM MCLEOD RAINE — Western novelist and charter member of the Western Writers of America.

NARD JONES — Journalist for the *Seattle Post-Intelligencer*, and author of 12 novels, including *Swift Flows the River*.

CHARLES LEWARNE — 1987 Washington Teacher of the Year, and author of various history books including *Washington State*, the leading high school textbook on Washington State history.

WILLIAM WILKINS — One of the judges who convicted leading Nazi industrialists during the Nuremberg war crimes trials.

JOHN CARLSON — Radio talk-show host and 2000 Republican candidate for Governor.

JENNIFER DUNN — 1959 graduate of Bellevue High School. Elected to the U. S House of Representatives in 1992, and was the first woman to run for House Majority Leader.

JIM TAYLOR — 1980 graduate of Bellevue High School. Screenwriter for the films *About Schmidt* and *Citizen Ruth*.

JANAMARIE HUPP — 1982 graduate of Bellevue High School. Television actor.

PETER KLETT — 1986 graduate of Newport High School. Guitarist for the band Candlebox.

JEFF BROTMAN — Founder of Costco Wholesale.

FRED DANZ — Founder of Sterling Recreation Organization.

BILL MUNCEY — Champion hydroplane racer.

TODD HOLLANDSWORTH — Graduate of Newport High School. 1995 National League Baseball Rookie of the Year, later went on to play left field for the Florida Marlins in the 2003 World Series.

JOHN OLERUD — Graduate of Interlake High School, and first baseman for the Seattle Mariners.

DON KARDONG — Olympic Marathoner and founder of Spokane's Bloomsday Run race.

PHIL NUDELMAN — CEO and President of the Hope Heart Institute and former director of the Group Health Cooperative of Puget Sound

Bellevue's population is 117,000 in 2002.

The *Eastside Journal* changes its name to the *King County Journal* in 2003.

Newsweek magazine chooses five Bellevue high schools — Bellevue, International, Newport, Sammamish, and Interlake — for its list of the top 100 high schools in America in 2003.

Bellevue celebrates its 50th anniversary in 2003 with a citywide 50Fest celebration.

Phantom Lake Elementary, the first new elementary school building in Bellevue in more than 30 years, opens in 2003.

Somerset Elementary undergoes a complete rebuild, and modernization projects begin at International School, Interlake High, and Sammamish High in 2003.

Bellevue's population dips slightly to 116,400 in 2003.

INDEX TO PEOPLE

INDEX TO PEOPLE